Attention:
People With Body Parts

With more than 50 parts and
pieces collected by Lexie Bean

ISBN: 0615718191
ISBN-13: 978-0615718194

Acknowledgements

I place my greatest gratitude towards every person and piece that gave body to this book.

In particular, I would like to thank: Sarah Bernstein for sending a Valentine to my feet; Katie Malone and Wes for showing me that bodies are limitless in love; Laura Grothaus for understanding my chaos; the writers of songs that make me feel whole and Yorrick Detreköy for giving songs to my mornings; Tails Williams for her spunky cats and soul; Zettie Shapey and Caroline Meister for dancing with my insecurities; the city of Budapest for uprooting a love of language, and David Tisel for witnessing it; the members of Horrible City BECAUSE I LOVE THEM; Will Shenton for collecting these words; Azra Karabegovic who walked me through conclusion after conclusion; my fellow high school rejects for raising me and Rosie Rae for raising me up; Chris Landers and Jake Kosinski who will have great karma; Shauna Godfrey and Shosh Gordon who have my favorite laughs; Mom, Little Yia Yia, and all of the women of my roots; and Jake Burns who reminds me that life continues through the people we have touched.

Attention: People With Body Parts

To those who find themselves on every page of my bones.

Attention: People With Body Parts

Attention:
People With Body Parts

(But, like actually)

Attention: People With Body Parts

Attention:

I was born a whole. A being that found sensation in every movement, sucked my toes in disbelief, cried when I felt it. There was perfection in my unbrushed hair; I could feel the wooden cradle sway with my every breath. I would open my eyes and the world would call me beautiful.

But then something happened. I became detachable: connected and layered with other bodies that time has made far from equal or whole. I started wearing shoes. Crying became weakness, split ends became laziness. My world boxed into schedules, and the rocking of a cradle and a mind transformed into mere fairy tales. Each day, it seemed difficult to open my eyes and call myself beautiful. The world would no longer do that for me.

At 9 years old I developed an eating disorder. Sprinkles, an extra 15 calories, filled my pockets for safekeeping. Sometimes I would cut my own hair and watch it fall to my sunken feet. Extra. Everything on and in my body felt like it was extra. Not knowing where to put these pieces, I abandoned the body that I had never felt at home in.

At 10 years old I picked up my first copy of J-14 Magazine. The great enlightenment! Life seemed better once I knew where to find a dress for the "perfect pear" shaped body and I had a pull out poster of Nick Carter and his frosted tips, teeth, and skin.

At 11 years old I discovered that my pearly white skin was the only thing keeping me safe in the whitest city in America.

Friends who left school, friends who were left behind. Difference negotiated their safety. And why was I different? You could see it in my pink finger tips. It was the reason I could walk the streets past 8PM ; the reason my below average reading level didn't land me in Special Ed. Ultimately, it was the reason I could move and have access to learn and maybe even speak. At the time, speaking was only for grownups. You know, the kind that wore nice business suits and pledged allegiance to the plastic blue sign "Families Still First" that marked the entrance the city. The kind of grownups that marked people who had skin color shades darker than blue.

At 12 years old I decided that I wanted to become a professional roller skater. With feet bound in leather boots, my leg muscles ballooned and wood burns became a life-style. I imagined my body spinning, moving, unraveling--guilt-free.

At 13 years old I got my period. I was wearing white pants and it was very stereotypical. However, puberty did not result in boobs or hips. Only my legs grew, and I earned the names Bean Pole, String Bean, and Bean Sprout. I almost enjoyed the new excuse to use puns as much as witnessing my male-bodied classmates' struggle with their clumsy new voices.

At 14 years old I slow danced with a boy to "Dare You To Move" by Yellowcard in a sweaty gymnasim. His red hands searching for my decorated waist, my wrists wrapped around his neck. I realized I like girls.

At 15 years old I started using Myspace. Someone told me it was the ultimate form of connection. It was the first time I could announce to the world when I was lonely, sneezy, pirate, cheerful, or any of the other seven dwarves. It was also the first time we took pictures of empty moments. As more girls documented duck faces in bathroom mirrors and friends' cats had their own profiles, I started to wonder with what species, exactly, I was connecting with. I suppose everyone deserves the space to say what's on their mind.

At 16 years old my fluid friends and I went through a spin-the-bottle phase. We often played in public with an emergency bottle someone would have in her Mary Poppins bag. This was as awkward as it sounds, especially when the mall security watched from their golf-carts.

At 17 years old I stopped shaving my leg hair. It felt nice, nicer than the actual hair. Friends made fun of me; some treated me as a personal petting zoo. Once upon a time, someone muttered "classless bitch" at its sight. It took me three years to finally write a love letter to my leg hair. We are very happy together.

At 18 years old a blue eyed someone called me beautiful for the first time since I had baby teeth. I was confused. I thought he was even more confused.

At 19 years old I relapsed. New York City introduced me to a world of burnt hair, high heeled feet, and robotic pouts (AKA modeling). We love you, they said. For your Bean Pole, Spring Bean, Bean Sprout self. Yes. But it was not enough. I needed to exchange three inches for a five year contract.

One inch gone: secrets shed off, scoops of frozen yogurt eroded.

Two inches gone: along with memory of feeling red hands on my waist and spinning, guilt-free.

Before I reached the goal of three inches, I broke the funhouse mirrors. The fragments served as souvenirs for how I will never again see myself. A voice can be bought, stretched, given privilege, put on display--but would always remained attached to my body. As it turns out, there are no photographs of empty moments. My legs recall what it is like to spin until my whole body floats. My lips still carry kisses of my spin-the-bottle friends, a police officer's grin, the swallow of a man's threats, the sip of a milkshake from a time I did not believe I was worth these words. Bodies overflow with stories and histories that take back the silence.

I gave up on modeling. An adult life of holding still became unappealing compared to moving, to speaking. Not the kind of speaking that pledges allegiance to the myth of family and plastic, but the kind that finds solidarity in being.

At 20 years old I was eating breakfast with four other American students in Transylvania. There was stubbled brown toast, plump red jam, and most importantly a pink table cloth that covered legs and bellies, regions that most Americans fear the most. One woman vowed, "When I go back to the States, my starvation diet will start." A wave of agreement and applause ensued.

One year relapse free and with a plate full of scrambled eggs, I quickly reached for my ribs to make sure they were cocooned under layers of skin and extra sprinkles. At that moment, I imagined empty bodies, empty homes; voices stretched and manipulated by the industry I almost served as a model for. I wanted to send letters to every home, not magazines with bizarre sex advice and photo-shopped identities. It would read: Beauty, World War Me is over. I, however, can never deliver such a statement alone.

This treaty requires compromise, a promise of safety, and it must come from within. A letter to ourselves is a folklore that grabs our roots and celebrates our stories and histories. It should be framed on the mantle and serve as a prayer before every meal. In response, I have challenged every person I know to write a letter to a body part.

As with embarking on a "starvation diet," or racial profiling in Michigan suburbia, one person's perception of his or her body impacts how everyone else self-constructs and self-destructs. These ideas under omnipresent pressures often influence what is beautiful and how many pieces of brown toast go untouched. Standards form, unrealistic standards form, and it has become difficult to determine whether insecurity is innate or contagious. To successfully tackle our individual body issues or rejoice our intricacies, others must also have the space to do the same.

The pieces featured in this book take on as many forms as it does perspectives, complexities, and safe-spaces. The standard letter, manifestos, and poems featured dissect each person's relationship with a body part that marks difference and consequence. Some confer shame, privilege, a desire for control of ability, color, and youth. Not all body parts are conventional or controllable. Multiple letters address disease and mental health that spills, latches onto soul, and breeds cancer. Other letters bring physical markers of experiences and human connection to light with scars and family ties. All of these parts replace time capsules and remind us that our bodies have fully lived. As long as our bodies live and layer, the journey continues and stories get longer.

The next time you see a left leg, an eyebrow, a deviated septum, remember they are all connected to:
the right leg, come-hithers, the wrinkled nose of your next girl,
the boys' locker room and
    spreadsheets,
fields long forgotten and the surrounding dirt, bruises in the mirror,

lines, Nervous-Father Syndrome, dental records, electric shocks,
dammed lakes and nail polish and pavement, swim suits,
    bowls of cereal, unlocked doors, family photos,
wanting to fall,
policing, clowning, word-games,
            thunder and fallen branches and ash and dust and
mornings,
    laughs and partners-in-crime, nose rings,
the county fair, fake smiles, jewels, and smoke,
    introductory physics class, a flat balloon
    machines, razors and bleach and ghosts, wanting to know
who's to blame,
black and blue,
    last Thursday, magical pills, thoughtful lips and chopped
wood,
eye contact and "I'm Sorry,"
    wanting to suck all the breath, birds,
    Kevin Bacon (and my mother)

These letters are for everyone, everyone with body parts and
everything that touches.

Attention: People With Body Parts

Contributors

This book contains one to three pieces/parts from the following people, listed in random order:

Eliza Diop, Chris Segal, Azra Karabegovic, Sarah Bernstein, David Tisel, Lexie Bean, Zettie Shapey, Christina Russell, Max Anzilotti, Anita Peebles, Julie Christensen, Tim McCarthy, Alyssa Kai Joseph Civian, Lolly Jane, William Passannante, Kevin Hu, Molly Rose Brennan, Kathy LaCombe, Jake Kosinski, Nicole Mak, Melissa Carey, Noah Voelker, Eileen Brucato, Karyn Todd, Bud Stracker, Noah Jones, Alice Beecher, Kelsey Scult, Sophia Bamert, Lena Amick, Alex Deeter, Laura Grothaus, Tails Williams, Katie Malone, Grant Gaston, Shoshana Gordon, Chris Landers, Eillie Anzilotti, Rachel Adler

Three participants wish to remain anonymous.

Attention: People With Body Parts

Dear Knuckles,

My friend is doing a project where she is having people write to different body parts. I thought for a while about which to write to. Knee? The cereal bowl part of the ear? Smallest eyelash? I settled on you, knuckles.

You remind me most of me. More than any other part. Even in the way you are sonically constructed. At first, knuckle is a goofy word. Sounds like chuckle or tickle. If you say it ten times fast, it sounds like a hen clucking. Silly. But then, slow down. Take you apart.
The kn- is gentle. Could be whispered. Could be kind.
The –u-… the –u- is the quiet space between the soft and the hard. The grey. The empty. The muted buzz. "I feel neither this nor that." The u will not stand up for itself in a fight. It won't kiss anyone's eyelids. It will just be.
And then the –ck. The glorious, rewarding, delicious, strong, horny –ck. It is the hard part of fuck. It is the shout of knuckle. It is probably the part of the punch that decides what shade of blue to paint the eye.

And then the –le. It rolls. It rolls the tongue, the word, the architecture of the hand. Rolling le. Rolling le.

I crack you often. Sorry if that is bad for you. Maybe I like pop rocks. Maybe I am a nervous person.

I clench you sometimes. I used to wake up because my fingernails would be digging into my palms. Excavating bones in a hand that wanted to be held.

I don't know if you noticed, knuckles, but I didn't use any possessive forms in the list of body parts. I guess this letter project has made me feel disconnected from the different parts that make my body my body. Are you really *mine*? Ownership is an odd concept. What have I done to deserve you? Maybe I should spend an hour a day reflecting on you, knuckles, and how much you do for me. I could substitute the time I spend on facebook with knuckle gratitude hour. But sadly, old friend, you and I both know that won't happen.

Attention: People With Body Parts

When did I stop speaking to my body? I used to dance. I guess now there is sex. But that is a dance for two people. That is a time for my knuckles to touch his knuckles and his hand to wake up my back and my lips to remind him that his shoulders exist. It is an incredible thing, knuckles. But I want something for just you and I. I want my joy, curiosity, fury, hunger, misery, idleness, fervor, and contentment to come and kiss every part of my body. Every peak and valley that you have sung into the tops of my hands. If I were explaining this to Cordelia, my favorite six year old, I would tell her I just want my insides to connect to my outsides.

Anyways, have a good day knuckles. I will try to take you on an adventure. I am supposed to be painting, but for some reason I haven't been able to lately.

Love always,

To my vagina:

We've always had a love/hate relationship.

We were alright growing up. Before puberty, we seemed to be decent with each other, but we had minor "kid" problems sometimes. Like when I wanted to buy a Jurassic Park licensed velociraptor toy. The other little girl and her vagina behind us in line made fun of us because you aren't a penis and we wanted a dinosaur toy. But that wasn't a big deal. We both knew dinosaurs were too cool to worry about someone making fun of us. Sure, too, there were other times we weren't allowed to participate in certain games, but they weren't usually games we were interested in anyway.

You made me a peeved often in our adolescence. We were banned from doing things we otherwise would have been able to do (if you were a damn penis) like going to my guy friends' homes and watching certain movies that were not "fit" for my fragile eyes. The first boy I really liked didn't like me back because you weren't a penis. I figured there must have been a legitimate reason for that; you were disgusting. A gaping wound not to be trusted because you somehow bleed for an entire week a month and never die. You were appalling.

We started to get past our differences when my dad kicked us out of his house. I started taking pride in the fact that I had you in my life. You and I belonged to a community. A sisterhood.

We are a woman. And that's the opposite of disgusting.

We let someone else inside for the first time at the age of 18. We discovered your amazing power to share emotions. Unfortunately, we also discovered your sensitivities. You are extremely prone to urinary tract infections At least we can both agree that this is inconvenient.

As we entered the real world, we found out about the discrimination we'd be facing. It's not pretty, but we know we're in it together and we can start a revolution.

We confirmed our suspicion at the age of 20 that we enjoy

interacting with other vaginas. The sensual touch of another woman and the ability to make her feel good was so gratifying to us. However, I discovered at this age also what heartbreak you vaginas can cause. I found out that someone else and her vagina were involved with my source of infatuation and his penis. We decided from that point on, we'd never let ourself be abused like that. We deserve to be treated with respect.

Not long after, I found love for the first time. We knew for the first time how it feels to be treated with respect and what it feels like to be touched by someone who cares about us. We love it so much that it hurts. It hurts so good.

And now we're struggling with the world and how the government is trying to control you, especially our ability to make love without having to worry about creating another human being or gain power politically. It's hard, but we're in this together. And we have a companion there with us who understands and back us up for once.

We got this.

With love,
Your partner-in-crime

Dear Lower Abdomen,

Time has had its way with you, I know. You and I are now 63, and here we are, still fighting the same battle (which you have always won). As I sat down to write this, you landed in my lap before my bottom even hit the chair. I know you find this comfy and convenient, but frankly, I'm sick of it. Worst yet, is the way you turn tying my shoes into an athletic competition. Yes, I always run out of breath before the job is done. You win.

Why must I always take you to try on new clothes? Can't I leave you home, just once? You love playing that mean joke – I look OK from the frontal view, and then turn sideways, and there you are, sticking out (with your buddies Muffin Top and Tushie). How many shopping trips have you ruined? And how many years have you made me stay out of the water for fear of appearing in public in a swimsuit? I can't even count them.

You know I have tried to win this battle between you and me. You know how many crunches I have done, how many diets I've tried. But you were always there, even jumping out over the top of my bikini when I was a 20-year-old size 0. Remember that? I almost can't.

Where did you come from? Really, I know. You were bestowed by your mother belly, and shared with your sister belly, and delivered to your daughter belly. Yes, I do think you are inherited like eye color or nose shape. How many generations have you lived in my family?

But alas, we are stuck with each other, and I suppose there are some positives to say about you. You housed my lady parts and ached when they announced they had reached full bloom into womanhood. You held the miracle that conceived and cradled two amazing new people, my babes. And now that those parts are retired, you are lovingly sheltering them like treasured keepsakes remembering lustier times.

Now that you have added a few more layers of "quilting," I will continue to do my crunches and diets, but I am again wearing swimsuits and my size 14s with…well, not with pride, but not with shame, either. You are a part of me, and like it or not, we are stuck with each other. Maybe, I should just accept you as a partner in crime.

Mr. Buttcheek,

Where do I begin? All these years, you've been my right hand man, always looking out for me when my back is turned. You have given me stability and stature when I am unsteady, and always there to lessen the damage after a hard fall. And when I was foolish and unafraid of the dark, you were there too. And it was you who suffered. When I looked at those bruises in the mirror the morning after, I thought of what you went through. Today, I still want to cry for you. I still see your scars, and I wonder if you will ever heal. Time hides the veiny scruffs and the bloody fingernail marks, but will your heart heal? Will your mind? I'm not sure if it is right to thank you for all that help, taking all of that damage. But I know deep down in my bones, I could never repay you. Because your strength saved me.

So here's to you, Mr. Buttcheek. Thanks for all the help.

Dear Fingernails,

Remember the days when you were so strong, growing quickly and beautifully with no cracks? I was always so proud to wear you naked, showing off your strength and pride. As the years went on, you started to crack. Your growth became stunted and you started to peel. I had to start hiding your flaws with polish, hoping I wouldn't see them either. As a child, I was strong and young and completely fearless, just like you, nails. As I aged with you, I too became cracked and flawed. The polish couldn't cover our imperfections. As I grow older still, I do not wear polish to hide you, but to show off a different beauty you can behold. I'm sorry it took me so long to realize your cracks and peels were beautiful and alive. I'm still coming to realize that my cracks and imperfections are beautiful, too. I think I'll start to go without polish.

Dear Spleen,

Why'd you have to break on me?

I know I really shouldn't have run down that hill, but I'm really sorry about it. I'm human, you know? We come flawed. We make decisions and sometimes the decisions we make become accidents that happen because accidents happen. I know I shouldn't have run down that hill but I wasn't trying to hurt you. I don't know what I was doing. I guess I wasn't thinking. Maybe I was trying to hurt myself a little bit, but not like this. I didn't want to fall. I should have known better, or thought more, but I'm sorry. I was just living my life because that's another thing about humans, we have a life to live. I didn't mean to hurt you while doing it. The thing is, I don't think I could do it without you. Please don't quit on me. I can't live if you do.

Love forever,

Attention: People With Body Parts

to my deviated septum

i remember the day we met so clearly. as if yesterday i was seventeen and a girl paused her kisses to tell me my nose was crooked. that night i turned my nose up at a mirror and there you were, a brash diagonal, a dandy on a lamp post doomed always to be merely "interesting looking," but wearing it well -- hat cocked on his head, cigarette dangling from his lips, diagonal grin. the sort i imagine you must have aimed at that girl the afternoon of your discovery, and which, in fairness to you, i imagine is usually more effective. you are the reason i can smell and breathe only through my left nostril, why mucus pools around my nasal cavity, why that girl's nose wrinkled in confusion, why boogers dry as winter lodge year-round in corners accessible only through unsubtle digging. but you are also the reason i rarely smell farts. so really i think we're about even.

In Praise of My Feet

I'm thinking about you fondly, my feet.

Sometimes, when we walk over the hot sand of a Lake Michigan beach and finally find ourselves in the cool shallows, where the waves have made little ripples of sand shining beneath the surface, or when we walk barefoot through tender grass to the base of a tree, I feel as if I am rooted to the very earth from whence we came. You are my roots, my torso is my trunk, my head and arms the branches of my verdant arboreal growth. Maybe there are little secret hairs on your underside, the same as the fungi have, sucking up every water molecule and nutrient cluster from the surrounding dirt, giving life so the roots can extend deeper and deeper into the ground.

You are completely flat, that if drafted, I wouldn't be able to serve in the army. So completely flat that the entirety of my sole is visible on the beach instead of the cute curvy outlines of others' footprints. You are skinny, so while I wanted to wear the fashionable cute shoes, my mom ordered Naturalizer sandals that old ladies wear in order to support my nonexistent arches.

You've had more injuries than any other part of me, even my heart. When I was seven years old, you stepped on a drywall screw but the platform shoes I had begged my mom to buy saved you—otherwise the rusty screw would have penetrated right through you! I remember crying in great pain in the emergency room from the metal protruding from you. On Christmas, the year I was eight, you got a sliver, a nasty chunk of wood thrust through your Christmas socks into my right big toe. Grandpa, my hero, dug the sliver out with only a few tears from me, but the sliver wasn't gone, and being from an old house with an old wood floor, your big toe got infected and eventually I went to the ER, where my 8 ½ month pregnant mother watched queasily as the doctor inserted a numbing shot right into my "owwee" and then proceeded to squeeze the pus out. That can't have been pleasant for you, and since then I've tried to be very careful with you. Even when I broke your toe in high school, and then when I was tap dancing and landed directly on the side of my foot and squished my bones together, resulting in a painful sprain, you still stood by me.

Attention: People With Body Parts

You, my feet, so delicate and slender, so fussed over, are the same ones I used to walk all over Europe, the same ones I dipped in Lake Superior every glorious summer in the north, and the same ones which a (former) boyfriend of mine said were ugly and misshapen (what did he know, with freckles AND red hair on his toes?)

You are the same feet with which I dance until you have blisters and seem to be falling apart, the same that I always dreamed would be one day wearing pointe shoes, the same that held me up when my knees buckled at my first kiss.

You have hiked through forests, enjoyed countless sandy beaches, have been in all five Great Lakes and three oceans and always remember being slightly stepped on when dancing with my dad at a Father-Daughter Valentine's Dance.

You have been tickled by my grandfather and brother, have kicked the door after a childish rampage, have had lake leeches burned off them, and have worn innumerable colors of toenail polish in hopes of being just as cool as the other girls.

You are the last thing to warm up when I crawl into bed, and you savor the delicious feeling of being entwined with someone else's.

I hope you walk down the brick walk for commencement proudly, and tread lightly but surely down a church aisle someday, and get to compare sizes with my child's footprint someday.

You were made to walk and travel and endlessly dance.

May you ever still be dancing in the dewed grass of a moonlit night,
Barefoot,
Sending roots down into the earth.

In admiration of your resilience and rootedness,

me

You Nose, You!

Oh nose, oh nose. I never thought I'd care about a body part as much as I do about you. Maybe 'care' isn't the right word. I think it's more like 'infatuate', 'obsess', 'TRIP'. Who knew I could place all my insecurities right inside you, and say that you are to blame on days when I don't feel as beautiful as I am. Is saying *"I'm sorry"* enough to make up for all I've put you through?

When I was young I used to rub my nose from side to side so much that my parents thought I had never ending allergies. My uncle always told me, "If you keep rubbing your nose like that you're going to get a big ol' line right across the bridge." I didn't listen to him. Rubbing my nose felt good! It was like an ever-persisting itch and I needed to scratch it! Well, eventually I got over it and the itch stopped coming. But, in it's place came a huge lump on the bridge of my nose. At the time, I didn't connect the dots between what I saw and what my uncle had foreshadowed. But as I got older and those teenage insecurities started rolling in, I kept questioning and looking for answers to why my nose had this big hump. I looked to family photos; was it in our genetics? I talked to doctors; is this something that can be surgically removed? Then I remembered what my uncle told me and I was crushed. I realized that all of what happened was my fault. Had I stopped rubbing my nose like a fool, maybe I wouldn't have this bridge here!

Of course, all of that made sense at the time. Looking back now though, I was crazy. It's incredible how we find ways to blame ourselves for things that are out of our control. I don't know why my nose is like it is, and perhaps it isn't important for me to know. But to focus all my energy on my nose, define my opinion about myself around my nose, and ultimately decide to flower or wilt based on my nose and other's perception of it, is absolutely crazy. In retrospect, I understand all of that but if I had been asked to write about my nose maybe even 4 or 5 months ago, I wouldn't have been able to even let myself begin.

Confidence is truly something that takes time and maturity. Even the prettiest faces are hiding the darkest insecurities and no one or nothing can mend them. That is because confidence is something that is born within and has to be grown from within as well. It's a matter of choosing whether to hold on to that pain and burden all your life, or choosing to accept your flaws and move forward. Maybe I got over my nose because I realized there are more important things in life like finding a damn job, graduating from Oberlin, having money and doing all of this while trying to keep my sanity as a Black woman. It could be that. But it could also be that I took a choice to let go and know that something as small as a nose cannot and will not affect my character, my success in life, finding a man (LOL), and being overall, happy. That was a choice I had to make on my own. If I had a penny for every time a person told to stop trippin' about my nose, I'd have a damn lot of pennies. But as I said before, confidence is born within and has to be grown from within as well. And like many things in life, the choice is yours.

I am happy to share this story about my nose not only because others can learn from it, but because I am finally able to let it go. Now that this secret is out of me, there is no reason for me to hold on to it anymore. If my nose is funny looking, let it be! Who am I to be upset that I'm not perfect? Striving for perfection isn't my place and it never will be. This life is quick but full of so much and energy should be directed wisely. Not towards being unhappy about noses, or body sizes, or feet, or hairlines or anything that God placed on our bodies and that we cannot change.

So, I can now comfortably say: *Dear Nose, I love you. Thank you for all that you are. Thank you for functioning so that I can breathe. Thank you for never being in the way when a ball comes to my face, or a door or anything of the like. Thank you for still being here for me even though I've just come to appreciate you. I love you for all your flaws and I promise I will never get a nose job to fix you. I know you are not a mistake and I am so grateful to have you. I love you nose and I love me too!*

To the fat on my stomach:

I've kicked this project around in my head for a while—21 years, now that I think about it—hoping to arrive at some grand realization of empowerment and confidence. Hoping to affirm what our parents and our teachers taught us, that we're all beautiful, despite everything around us screaming the contrary into our faces. Hoping to become a more mature man, less crippled by doubt. But this is all I have: I'm tired.

My whole life I've been looking down at you with nothing but shame. It was like staring my inferiority in the face, a scarlet letter for the 21st century. I've always seen you as a symbol of what I'm not—a star athlete, popular, attractive, what have you. And now I'm done.

Despite my initial intentions, I'm not writing this to tell you that I've had a revelation, that I don't need you anymore, that you can go to hell (though at times that still seems awfully nice.) I'm writing this to tell you that I'm just exhausted. I'm not who I was when I was 10, the kid getting mocked in the boys' locker room. I'm a grown man now, with loving friends and family, and to tell you the truth I just can't afford to waste any more time on it.

So instead of looking down at you and seeing a symbol of what I'm not, I choose to look down at you today as a symbol of what I am—all of those perfect Thanksgivings with one too many slices of apple pie; the enormous love my Italian family has given me in the only way Italians know how; those wonderfully greasy omelets with my grandfather on a Saturday morning.

Sure, there will be moments when I want to rip you right out of me. I'm not that strong yet, and maybe I never will be. But in those moments I'll remember this: I love you, from the bottom of my heart. Because without you I simply wouldn't be me, and it turns out that me isn't such a bad thing to be anymore.

To my Hips (and dear Thighs)

I say now I love you,
I know I didn't always show it.
Too young, too skinny, where are your boobs girl?
I remember feeling you were off
Wrong
Why couldn't I be like all the girls around me?
When was I going to be like all of them?
What is going *on* down here?
Mom said, "men like hips"
But what were *these* hips doing on me?
I felt so foreign with you,
Why can't all this be in my bra.
Even exercised every day for two months to make you skinnier
More my own
Make myself "balanced",
So many years later I still comfort and criticize you
Makes a woman out of me
Or an object
Or a jewel?
Hips, it's taking me almost two decades to fit you
But I'm still "too skinny" from the outside
You're not a pear! You're too small. Now that girl, is a pear
Can no one see you can still be petite and unhappy with yourself?
Oh Thighs,
Dear Hips
When I look at you
You've got me asking,
Where am I, in all of *this*?

To: the creature in my chest

You're not something that's exactly a part of my body, at least certainly not a visible one, or even an understandable one, but you're something that's always been there—a weight that has always been there. I even sometimes think, you're what I really used to cry about when I was a baby—the weight that just sits on my chest. That I was screaming and crying at the top of my lungs for someone to explain to me what the feeling was that I could not understand. Would never fully understand. Some days you're small, isolated, almost even forgettable or manageable, and some days you eat away at my stomach, tingling into my toes, and filling my chest with so much tension I can't tell if it's exploding, imploding, or constricting every last breath from my lungs. But whatever the case, you have definitely become a part of my body, or maybe more like a creature of my body. Because you sure are, your own living, breathing, *creature*.

You are the creature of anxiety and fear that I now learn, thanks to my fancy education, is the result of big words that stand for even bigger ideas. The systems and actions of patriarchy, colonization, genocide, heteronormativity, inequality, injustice, and many more that wreck havoc on communities. Making it so that I learn and feel that I'll never live up to an impossible ideal, never make the right choice or feel the right way, say or not say the right thoughts—that ultimately, none of us will or can.

You are the one who eats away at my friends whose lives are already made unequal by the hands of white supremacy and by the hands of heartless beliefs policing identities. You become one's personal and very own creature—birthed through the genocide of millions of people, birthed through the enslavement of people of color's bodies and of differently abled bodies, birthed through forgotten histories and languages of indigenous peoples. I see, we all can see, there are more of you creatures breeding at faster and faster rates, eating away at more and more people.

You are the creature of anxiety and fear that I now learn seems to be passed down through genes, through generations—you are the creature of anxiety that ate away at my dad until he became addicted to alcohol and xanax, and I guess has now found my petite, 5' 2'' body.

***

However, as immobilizing as you can be (especially in the mornings when I wake up with an overwhelming sense of dread and impending doom), you have also given me a gift—that of empathy, of understanding, of open-mindedness.

Because I guess in some way, you allow me to see and feel past my own privilege and security—to feel the fear and recognize the power of injustice at the hands of external powers. You're my own double-edged sword of sorts. You make me feel what needs to be felt, but afraid to say what needs to be said. You create an earthquake of nerves when the time comes for me to speak. My thoughts a whirlwind of confusion and blurred insecurities—lost inside a tornado attempting to grab at any familiarity.

***

So when someone asks me, how do you get rid of your anxiety? Well creature in my chest, you know this answer better than any, because you make it so I have no fucking idea. I wish I could tell them something. Love? Music? Dancing? Yoga? Meditation? Chocolate? They all eventually become band-aids within such an ailing world.

***

And you know what? This letter to you isn't perfect. It will never be perfect. And I finally realize that's the point. The first thoughts that spill out of my fingers are as meaningful as those that require hours of crafting. I need to combat the perfectionism that feeds you, that feeds into your heaviness on my chest. The perfection. The competition. The need for control that separates us all. Forcing us to live in solitary confinement with creatures like you in our chests.

And well, I'm tired. I'm only 21, and I'm tired of waking up everyday tired, and no matter how much I sleep being tired. I'm done with the fact that even the simple task of speaking up in class, of asking someone a question, or calling someone on the phone, can work my nerves up into such a frenzy that I feel like passing out.

So, creature in and on my chest. This is to you. You will always live with me, but you will not always live for me. I promise you that.

Yours truly, with growing understanding.

Attention: People With Body Parts

When I was little I used to think there were children living in my
lungs, their small hands tearing up the fibers of my ribcage, the
instrument of my body strange and out of tune, like someone had
plucked a hole in that sweet spot between the sternum and the
heart, planted a stop sign in front of my feet made of ash and
blackbirds, so that I never ran faster than the sweet swinging of
crickets slumming through the crabgrass in june

asthma
my grandmother died in a wheelchair
under the weight of your clutch
please don't wrap your hands
so tight 'round my throat

you are no monster
you are a child
you beat beneath my bones
with tiny fingers

Toes,

I love how you twinkle.

Admiringly,

Dear uterus,

I guess I should say I'm sorry. I feel obliged, but really, I'm not sure I am sorry. I'll confess that ever since the diagnosis, every time I squat to pee I stand up a little tentatively, like you are a thin glass I dare not grip too tightly. Like the infection might slither out and I'd have to *see* it. I'm afraid it would look like my mother.

It's not a question of whether or not I feel guilty. I'm just not even sure that this infection, which made the doctor's finger feel like a sharp nail when it touched you, is even about you. Or maybe you should be apologizing to me.

Dear ovaries,

I want you to know that I have dreams in which I am pregnant. I want you to know that I wake up from these dreams feeling like I swallowed the world. Never, in my hazy state, do I question where the baby is, who the father might be, and how his sperm snuck past the defenses of my copper T. I have the baby; it is mine.

I move about my dreams as an open cradle, an abundant basket, a mussel shell half open and purple rimmed, filled with the briny sea. I feel beautiful, like a lighthouse. In spanish the phrase for giving birth is "dar a luz": literally, to give to light. It is as if, while in the womb, the baby belongs to my own universe of darkness and when I push them through my throbbing vagina, I hand them over to the whims of the world's merciless light.

I wake now to the same gingerness of gestures but the dream is twisted, slapped together wrong. I am not pregnant, luckily, but neither am I welcome to myself. Is it dramatic to say I've been invaded? I've never been infected where such a dream resides.

Dear vulva,

The day I found out I had genital warts, I went home and painted my fingernails red. The air was electric and crumbling; I wanted to do something loud. I remember the way the Pacific looked out the bumpy bus window on the ride home -- an incorruptible blue. The red nail polish looked indecent against my flesh, like a weapon.

A month later when I found out I had Pelvic Inflammatory

Disease, a bacterial infection often caused by chlamydia, I ran a bath and shaved my legs for the first time in seven months. Thick vegetation flushing away in little black clumps-- clockwise, in the northern hemisphere, down the drain. I remember asking my lover Marco if my body hair bothered him. We were lying on my bed in Chile, his scarred and calloused hands tugging at the thick black strands beneath my bellybutton. I knew most Latinas were fastidious with their body hair, but mine didn't seem to faze him. He answered in the negative: "you wouldn't be you without it."

Now a world away, with all my soapy hair down the drain, I looked at my naked legs. They just looked like legs, and they still looked like mine. I went back to bed.

Dear fallopian tubes,
I hope I'm not infertile.
Dear womb did you ever think you look like a plastic bag? i've never seen you before, just the medical diagrams on wall while waiting for the doctor, and then once my ovaries in an unltrasound. a nice big triangle tinged with colored pencil pink. little sacks connected by tubes with only one slimy exit. i think of a lagoon fed by an underground stream. just a trickle and otherwise, still water. perfect for breeding mosquitos, you know? the lagoon, i mean.
but we were talking about a bag. just, you know, a trash bag. for trash. mini muffin cups broken soap dishes gnawed off shoelaces banana cores chunks of change rotten meat warm cardboard batteries toothbrushes phone cords cantaloupe rinds. it's not just that it's got no use, it's that nobody wants it. nor just disrespected, but not deserving of respect. *that's* what makes it trash.
in valparaiso chile there's a flea market every sunday. vendors set up their rows of blankets on avenida argentina in the shadow of the congreso and the giant statue of copper wire. a few bring umbrellas to protect from the heat but the rest just sit out on their tired blankets, displaying what the 90s spit up. childrens books skeleton keys plastic animals used sneakers grandma's blender samsung phone chargers barbie heads eyeglass cases corduroys quinientos pesos quinientos! you thought you'd forgotten all that stuff and then there it is, in your womb, looking washed out from the mid-morning sun. in the shadow of copper wire, a

symbol of national progress, the trash from the past turns out to not biodegrade so quickly. throwing it out doesn't make it disappear.

Dear cunt,

We liberals do not speak of sin. Civilized folk on the precipice of reason, we tailor dirtiness and darkness in garments called "responsibility," "precaution," "respect." That way we can talk about "irresponsible behavior" and not have to say, you did this to yourself. We can ramble on about the importance of self respect and never have to utter the words "dirty whore." In the world of thinly cloaked Christian morals, punishment falls swift and just on the deserving, and the logic screeches in reverse: I am punished, therefore I deserve it.

But we all know it's your fault, you selfish dirty cunt. What the fuck were you thinking? Only of your ravenous gaping mouth needing to be fed.

Dear reproductive system, a post script:

So yesterday the test results for gonorrhea and chlamydia came back negative. So PID must have come from some other bacterial infection--maybe not even sexually transmitted, just some little germs that decided my pussy looked pretty good to crawl into. An entirely reasonable response.

The antibiotics would wipe away any disease along with the infection, so the results shouldn't matter -- except that they do. In the test lies the difference between an accident and a betrayal. It determines whether I'm with you or against you, whether I got unlucky or you did. Whether the infection is a bummer or a deserving consequence. That's why everyone wants to know. They don't want medical answers; they want to know who's to blame.

But here's my diagnosis: at no point in the last six months did I stop loving you. At no point in the last six months did I stop loving me. A severe case of unconditional love, and I see no reason to stop.

Mouth:
I can't see you without a mirror but thank you for being twisted and topsy-turvy so if I die and am too fucked up to recognize, they can use my dental records. Thank you for yellow straight smiles and spluttering stutter starts. For curvy gum joints and blood trickles in the sink. For dog longue tongues and faint grey moustaches and wobbly singing. Thank you (and fuck you) for taste.

Attention: People With Body Parts

my semaphores

—even if uneven
before i even
remember words—

you pronounce
my come-hithers
which is why

though it hurts us
i must deprive you
of a few
extra
hairs

Dear Spine,
You are the sap spring
            the spigot of nerves,
which I drain for sound, an image
of linked fragments,
            calcified from a pinprick. Diaspora
of soul, I name you the home
I can never reach,
            the space of skin above you. I ask
                    someone to scratch, to crack.
            You are the midst of muscle pain,
thread of brain, you are so full of stories
in the way of any skein of flesh,
            in the way my breasts are the night
                    of the hypnotist and the boy,
                    who looked me in the eye
                    when he said he liked small chests
                            (as if that were an accomplishment)
                    and I said *me too*.
            My feet tell of running to blisters,
                    dreams of being chased.
            My blood is the end of every poem,
                    heavily ironic—
in the homunculus of my words,
            I would draw large teeth and small heels, hips
            full to overflowing and dust
                    where my eyes should be.
                        A visceral hierarchy.
                            Let me speak about the
                    revolution and evolution
                        of my hands, the way nails and hair
                            continue to grow after death,
                        my mole
                            reminds me of a kiss, and
                        my knees
                                    belong to
                        fourth grade fears, when I
                        thought them dimpled
                            as potatoes.

And always there was you,
oh spine,
a slippery strand pulled to each
small purpose, dribbling a myth:
Accept that you are deserving of the space you take up
in the world.

Dear feet,

When you first made your appearance in the world, your little heels were so slim, they didn't look like they would work! Dad was so concerned that he asked the doctor if I would ever walk (yeah, I think half of that was Nervous-Father-Syndrome). Twenty-one years have passed and you went from just a couple of inches to wearing a women's size 9 (and yes, you are welcome for all the beautiful shoes I put on you). Through those years, I have put you through a whole lot more than just high heels.

You always seem to carry the brunt of my ridiculous clumsiness. It was when we were eleven when the first toe was broken and several more have followed. Thirteen was when we tore that ligament and walked around in a cast for a while. And it was only this Christmas when I almost sliced the tendon in your big toe when I dropped the shower door on you - gold medal clutz effort right there. Of course, these are only the hospital visit injuries. I always seem to cover you in bruises or scrapes of some sort.

I guess in a way, this is an apology letter. I love you. I really really do. I love that leftie has an extra bone, because, well an extra bone is so cool. I love when we point our toes, I can see just about every tendon. I love that the last two little toes curl, while the others are straight (it's like a combo of Mom's straight toes and Dad's curlies!). You take me everywhere I want to go: climbing up mountains, dancing across stages, diving into pools and walking around the world. I am sorry for not appreciating you enough and for not protecting you better.

But to be honest, you have some things to fix too. You crack. All. The. Time. Apparently that's kinda bad? I'm not really sure about that, but it's loud. And it's awkward when you crack when the room is quiet. So please just like relax on that ok? Also, whenever I jump around, your ankles are slacking. Every time I jump too hard, it feels like you are gonna fall off. I know how exhausted you get when you go on long walks, but please just hang in there a bit better?

We've been through a lot together. And while we have changed and gotten bigger, some things haven't changed: your slim heels and my propensity to knock you up. I promise to take better care of you (lotion!) if you take care of me. Together, I think we have a few thousand more miles and six decades life. Thanks for carrying me around; love you guys.

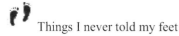 Things I never told my feet

1. You. Bulbous and round and useful. Like little elves. I could like you. Honestly, I have never before thought about my feet. You— my feet— are not my priority; further from that you are not quite me. And ask around, I'm not disconnected from my body. Maybe you know that.
How should I know?
Of course.
Of course you are my body.
But You. Are simple.
I walk,
Of course. So effortless.
I run. I used to ice-skate when I was 10 until I unintentionally crashed into a wall and the bleach-haired Russian instructor made me skate, crying and embarrassed, around the rink by myself. Since then, I've learned to strut. Not high-heeled chest out (though in seventh-grade purple stilettos highlighted polka dotted skirts and neon tube tops). Now I have mastered walking with queer, quiet pride. Low-key, back and forth, eyes-wide.
Still.
This is what I mean. You don't make my walk. You keep me balanced, keep me up. Up.
But you don't make my walk. I want to say I like you, but—

2. When I get sleepy everyone knows—I don't capsize like Mel or, like Dad, subconsciously mumble "said the midget" in the middle of bedtime stories. Instead, my feet come out. Little nibblers. I rub and hold each toe; pacified.

3. Please remember (a helpful guide):
    • Standing toes-curled for too long makes the middle pad-part cramp. These shooting pains might last for hours or days.
    • Walking in a straight line is neither inventive nor practical. Fuck them all.
    • Useful tools for seduction. Sticking cold ones under someone's butt is the perfect silly tool for meet, greet. Will break the don't-touch-me ice.
    • Too hot water feels good but it still burns.

- Multiple slaps will not get rid of a "pins and needles" spidery sleep. When this happens, move with caution. Falling down stairs is not particularly fun.
- Just the phrase *toe sucking* sounds gross. The very opposite of *cellar door.*
- This little piggy went to market (giggle). This little piggy went home (ehaa). This little piggy went wee(!) wee(!) wee(!) All the way home.

4.   Size Five (or) Proof of the Things Gone Wrong
At five feet, people will ask- can I pick you up? You are cute, they coo. They don't speak of you. I am meant to be sweet and flexible. Pick me up and you will find a round butt, broader shoulders, and size EIGHT. Yes, you kept growing past my sister's. Past the girl with the red hair. She who is taller, not broader but longer. But has curves too. And little little hands and little little feet.

5.   Do…. You know that time I went up and down and you stayed put—gladiator sandals framing your curves and slamming—kicking—pushing—curling—and the shoes! Still on… We did good.

6. You look like old men- very wrinkly and translucent and veiny; unwanted hair and unknown discoloration. And rough edges.

7.   The immeasurable delight I took in head-to-foot toe biting. Oh yes! It was great! Each rip was- well- caused no real harm to the friends. A little bleeding, some pain. Practically intentional. The toes, the knuckles, the bones, and those long stretchy elegant tendons. Every time I look at those tendons I wonder:
        a. How strong they really are
        b. What it would be like to chew on them

    I imagine that if I were to actually eat you up- Yes, if I were to really full on eat you, the tendons would be my least favorite part. I imagine you would really taste like gristly meat. I could post an ad on Craigslist and find someone to share you with me.

chicago craigslist > personals > women seeking women

all chicago | city of chicago | north chicagoland | west chicagoland | south chicagoland | northwest indiana | northwest suburbs

women seeking women

search for: in: women seeking women ⊙ title only ⊙ entire post [Search]

Poster's Age min max ☐ has image

[w4w forum] [parental control software] [**search keyword** [STOP PIPA (S 968) and SOPA (HR 3261)!!!] [**AVOIDING SCAMS & FRAU**]

Hungry? - (city-north)

Can you help? - 37 - pic

Shimmering in white - 19 - pic

"Looking for dinner-buddy. Tonight. Main Course: my feet. If you do or ever have had cannibalistic tendencies or are curious about tasting human flesh or just want to eat my feet- please reply. *FOR REAL!* My feet are not particularly attractive, but seem to be meaty. (would be down for some pre-dinner foreplay. DTF.)"

Let's call the respondent Ari. With whatever we had, we'd chop off left. Maybe Ari would be more prepared—chainsaw? We could use steak knives and gnaw at the bone until it split. In olive oil with rosemary, I'd wince and smile and chew.

8. I will nurture the kicks of my little belly-babies. I know that each push, all that pressure, will bring me up and down. And this I promise (you) I will not judge the bulbous and round. I will recognize the useful as beautiful. I will kiss every fucking toe on your feet and cry at your laugh.

To My Teeth,

I believe we need to reconsider our relationship. I have, for a while, tolerated the pain you inflict upon me, because I felt it was part of our gentlemen's contract – you turn solid foods into tiny, digestible pieces, that makes all the other parts of my body quite pleased. You convert the food into the bits which the tongue can easily morph into taste sense, which then the brain interprets as pleasures, which then improves my wellbeing. In return, I allowed you to press pain unto me and I always said "no pleasure without a little pain! Without contrast how could one even discern between all the pleasure food gives them? No, a little pain enhances every good feeling." I sat quietly through years of Dr. Roland driving his screaming drill into cavities; I remained still through long root extraction procedures; I even wore braces for several years with some amount of grace. However, last Thursday, you thrust force your final insult by reliving my mouth of tooth #19! I was on such a lovely drive through the woods, of this fine state of Texas, when you felt it was appropriate to evacuate that tooth and spoil the remainder of my day. That gross injustice was uncalled for: I have brushed you, flossed you, and washed you, all in the vain hope that you would at least stay in my head where you had been placed! If you persist in fleeing from my mouth, I will drive ahead with full force and remove you all myself! This is not a threat; it is a promise of mutually assured ruin. Do not force my hand teeth, for the blow will be swift and without mercy.

Respectfully,

Dear Left Leg,

What's up with you? You hold me up, but just barely. Like when I run for long mileage you fail me, making Right Leg and Right Hip sore from bearing most of the weight. But I care about you man! I worry about you. Right leg is fine, strong, reliable, ze'll make it on zir own. But you man! You are a part of me. I need you too. Just talk to me! Lately looking at you I see you're sickly, weak, and thin – dull and imprecise in your movements.

I feel like you are isolating yourself from me. Sometimes I don't even feel your pain. You'll be slamming the pavement beneath my body for an hour, not helping me along, not really there at all and then all of a sudden next day you're stiff and it hurts to walk on you. We have *got* to learn to communicate better. Right leg gets sore when ze's tired. That's good. That way I know not to keep slamming zir on the ground until ze's ligaments and tendons tear. You don't want that do you? I don't. I need you. Did I mention that already?

Anyway it's not just you man, but also all of y'all   left-side crowd. You guys are moving away, growing more distant, though we appear connected on the outside to everybody else. Giving me stabbing electric shocks in my neck every so often. You used to take me places. Now… We simply walk alongside each other.

We're friends, totally still friends. I mean for sure. But I love you… I mean I know we used to love each other. Right? No I'm sure we did. We totally did, and I still love you now. But like, I'm not sure. I mean I am sure. Sure that you… and I and I'm sure…we'll make it.

Yours truly,

P.S. You should know I love you and I promise we'll go see all different kinds of clinicians. You've been talking about that for a while now. I should be a better listener. I know I've been skeptical, but, well… I don't know if you know, but I'm going to start medical school soon. I'm becoming a doctor! That way we can learn more about each other. Be best buds and more. Take a chance on me?

Dear Hips,

I'm not sorry about the bruising. I mean, yeah, I am, but I'm not. Occupational hazard, nahmean? It's not even like they're that big - let's say a quarter-sized patch of permanently discolored skin on the same place, port and starboard.

Every job affects your body in a different way, dude. Like lactation consultants. Bet you five dollars a lactation consultant has carpal tunnel or calloused fingertips or something from flicking so many obstinate nipples. That's how you get a new mother to lactate, right? By flicking? Maybe? Whatever.

Not like you're the only guy getting dinged, either. Shins have it particularly bad, and Left Heel just got over a bruise from that time I was dangling upside down from the rehearsal room ceiling pipe and barefoot gainer dismounted to concrete. That shit hurt.

Actually, I hope you're proud of the bruises. I am. They mean I've been pratfalling enough to (hopefully) legit know stuff. I've fallen more times in more ways onto more surfaces than you might have thought possible. Hell, it's gotten to the point where if someone pushes me off balance and I hit the deck - all of this by surprise - I'll almost certainly be fine. It's a pretty awesome super power.

Clowning is hard, dude. Physical comedy is hard. Turns out pratfalling, no matter how good you are, isn't free. No pain, no gain. So thank you, Hips, for putting up with me and the things I do. Because clowning - the modern kind I practice, the kind that's a combination of standup, improv, cartoon logic, and sound-manipulation (none of that Barnum and Bailey shit) - is one of the ways I express and hopefully spread my joy about being alive. It's one of the tools I use to try to incite the humor response in my fellow human beings. I think that's worth a bruise or two, don't you?

Love,

Journal of a Mad Ornithologist-Cellist

Dear Left Hand,

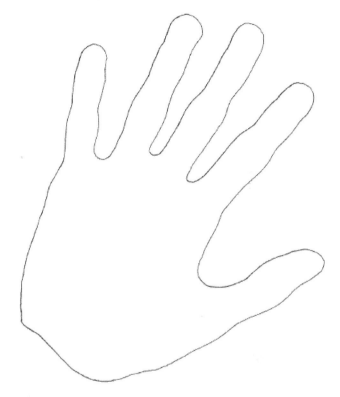

I guess I've never taken time to write you before. You glide across the keys, in tandem with Right Hand, ever vigilant, making my thoughts possible—or maybe not my thoughts, but their exercise—their physicality.

So has been your fate throughout our lives. But I hope for all the menial tasks you've had to accomplish at the behest of my will, for all the times you've been covered in bird poop, or bitten by cardinals, or shoved in thorn bushes on a blind, groping search for Gray Catbird nests—I hope you have had joy as well. The soft, delicate sensation of robin eggs surrounded by their nest, although you don't know "nest," only the feel of grass and mud and thorns. You are blind to their sky blues and turquoises—to their speckles. But I also am blind until you, with dexterity and finesse, extract them from the nest and bring them into my world: my sight, my understanding, my profession.

As often as you deal with birds now that I'm an ornithologist, you have spent long hours practicing cello—following the impulses of my brain but working relentlessly to learn the fingerings, the muscle memory. But then, as with the first touch of eggs hidden deep within the nest, a performance—the audience, the warmth of the stage lights, the sweat and sliding up and down the metal strings—and you are all they can look at. A whirr of contractions, of pressure, of vibrato—intricate, passionate, and powerful.

Through you I feel the world. Yes, 'feel the world'—it has a nice ring to it. Oh, no pun intended! But you never wore those anyway. Always free, unrestrained. Some might say unadorned. But I think you were and are pure. As you brown in the sun, the tiny hairs bleach and turn to gold in the summer rays: may you know one iota of my great thankfulness for all you do—and all you've done without me ever giving you a second thought. I'll keep your nails trimmed and I will keep you strong. For now, before I turn to sleep, take a moment: relax and know that you are beautiful.

To my right hand:

Our bond goes way back. We developed it in our initial five years, when I sucked on your first two fingers like most little kids suck their thumbs. It changed us; those fingers still feel different to me, odd in a way I can never accurately describe to others. They're kind of tingly, maybe more sensitive. They've held on to the instinct to suck them. But despite that subconscious sensation that we've got a continued shared connection, I now neglect the prominent role that you play in my life.

So this is a thank you, but also an apology. I so depend on you, but rarely do I acknowledge all the work that you do for me. Instead, I tell stories about you as a way of defining myself, taking advantage of only your distinctive characteristics. I envision you as an entity separate from my moving, living body; you're a freeze-frame image burdened by the symbolism I confer upon you.

There's your crooked pointer, inherited from mom. My left hand has this too, but it's nevertheless an important aspect of your unique personality: the finger straight up to the third knuckle, then the top section both twisted in toward the middle finger and bent to the right to point at it. I only noticed this about you, and that it was somewhat unusual, in my pre-teen years. Now each time I look at you for longer than a passing glance, I acknowledge your crookedness with a hint of recurring surprise.

Despite that more recent discovery, I've long been aware that you display physical manifestations of my own personality. Riding the bus home from elementary school one day after having had art class, I spotted a muddy blue welt underneath the nail on your ring finger. In just our first couple years writing you had developed your callous, which always became particularly prominent after drawing with markers. That callous demonstrates how you chose to hold the pen with your first two fingers rather than with just one, as the teacher had taught us to do; it also must have grown—and never gone away—because I send you all my tension, which you then press into the pen.

I also love to tell people about the little triangular scar on your lower back, just above the wrist. It's faded so much that sometimes I have to double-check to make sure it's still there. Remember that day, back in third grade, when Rebecca was telling me how her older brother had cried when she scratched him, and suddenly she reached out and scratched me to show me that it doesn't hurt? As the skin tore off, bright red blood welled up at the surface, even then in the distinct shape of a right triangle. I'm sorry about that—I remember well the burn from her nail, and how I fought against even a single tear—but I'm also sorry for taking so much pleasure in the scar when it did form. My best friend will always be with me, etched into my skin, I thought, which is why I repeat that story year after year. (Clearly I still buy into that kind of nostalgic thinking. Though in reality you and I are both in constant states of flux. I was littler then, so I'm not sure how big the scar originally was, but it's now shrunken to a size not much bigger than a pinhead, and you can only tell that it's raised because of that faint shadow outlining its edges.)

As you can see, when I think of you in terms of these descriptions, I fail to recognize that you're more than a body part easily accessible for study and objectification—you're an extension of my arm, a piece of the subject me as well. I realize how much you do for me when I tell people about how I type: with only my two pointers, your pointer responsible for the right two-thirds of the keyboard (that's how dominant, how much stronger than my left hand you are). My reluctance to learn to touch type is another pretty quirky part of me that you embody; if I may say so myself, we get along just fine the way we're doing it.

So thank you for typing and handwriting thousands of pages, millions of words for me. And for brushing my teeth, combing my hair, unlocking doors, applying makeup, holding onto the straps of my purse as I walk, shaking others' hands, feeding me finger foods, turning pages, grabbing on to railings, scratching my itches, carrying bags of groceries, zipping my zippers, and performing all those other tiny daily tasks that must accumulate. I hardly ever think of them, or acknowledge that you're doing them. I rarely think about being right handed. And when I do talk about it, or reflect upon the many tasks that my hands carry out for me, that image of the crooked-fingered, calloused, scarred hand—of you as you are—doesn't come to mind. Instead it's just a generic, uninteresting hand, like out of a picture book or on a plastic doll, there to do what hands do.

Having taken the time to address you personally, I'm sure I'll now see you in a new light. Not all the time necessarily, but more often, will I put two and two together and notice that while you are that fascinating object, a record of my life, you're simultaneously an integral player in the living of my life. My life does act upon you, giving you callouses and scars for me to define myself by, yet you're not devoid of your own agency, and I'd be having a harder time getting by without you and the work you do.

I've long since outgrown the need for comfort from your first two fingers. But know that I do still take comfort in who you are and how much you help me. In the most basic sense of it, I experience the world through you, through your touch.

They say that hands most accurately reveal a person's age, so I know there are many changes in store for both of us. With my newfound regard for you, I'll look out for the ways in which you age, I'll try to accept them and not immediately stereotype or romanticize them. And if one thing does remain the same, I bet it'll be that dormant childhood instinct to suck your fingers.

Love.

Dear Belly,

When I was ten, me and Ma turned my belly button into an eye. I'm sure you remember--it was a very serious surgery. I lay on my back on the sandy flowered couch in Florida and tried not to shriek as Ma lifted up my shirt with her cold hands and bit her lip to concentrate. She bent over me and used the newly-sharpened tip of her eyeliner to create, right there on my squirming moonshine skin, a pupil and iris and lashes and lid. Then she kissed my new eye, exactly in its middle. I was impressed and Ma was impressed and my brother was jealous because his looked only like a navel. Mommy tried to make his belly button a mouth but I smiled because it still looked like a navel, only dirty.

I liked you then, Belly, as something to play with, to form into doughnuts and bagels and silly-looking big fat lips. But I did not like you as an extension of my body. Your smooth full paleness did not inspire confidence or that warm swelling that means I am happy or have just drunken hot soup. I did not love the lines that crept along your sides, a result of my refusal to sit up straight, or the hairs that ran from my third-eye-belly-button down towards my girl-place. I hid you under layers of tanktops, I sucked you in while I walked. I hated you, with an active, acidy hate that I only also felt for the girl who made fun of my leg hair in gym class. I remember being in kindergarten, standing in front of the full length mirror after my bath, wishing you were flatter like Charlotte's was and thinking you looked kind of like those starving Africans I saw on television once. I remember looking at mama's belly while she changed and knowing mine would continue to be round, a fixture as enduring as our family's curvy toenails or love for word games.

As I moved towards the beginning of middle school and was still angry at you, Belly, you got fed up with my bullshit, and you started talking back. This was a surprising and unpleasant occurrence. I involuntarily formed a habit of barfing each time I kissed someone new, or before I got to the airport. It became your favorite means of communication to bequeath unto me horrific stomach aches before every test, big decision, or speech I gave. And as a special treat every so often, you used the guerrilla tactic of surprisearrhea to really drive home your thoughts. It was like you were my conscience or my mom or something, embedded in my torso in the most unpleasant of ways. You told me everything that I did not want to hear but still knew deep down in my digestive tracts. I wanted to be a regular teenager and make regular teenager mistakes. I wanted a regular-person belly, the kind of belly that was a silent and complacent co-conspirator. But you, Belly, stood your ground. And I am so very thankful. Because though my adolescence was filled with much too much spandex and unpleasant bodily functions, you made me listen to myself, and hard. You made me listen when I knew something was wrong and when I knew something was right, and you made me listen to that burgeoning peep that told me that you were, in fact, a wise and beautiful built-in friend.

I think a big part of me growing to love you slowly, Belly, was going to sleepaway camp. You know the place-- crunchy-hippie-Jewy-happy-deliciousness. We felt happy there, and safe. EXCEPT for the showers. My camp had a shower system designed, I think, to make insecure tweens face their bodies head-on. All the girls showered together, in one little room with not enough spigots on the wall or soap on the shelves. All these sudsy naked bodies were so close together, there was no way to not acknowledge the puberty abounding, the awkward and gangly and pudgy all in one tight space. I was so uncomfortable with this arrangement, and with my body, that first year that I would wake up at five in the morning and shower by myself so as not to encounter others. And then one morning, two other girls appeared with the same plan in mind. I was trapped. And I showered there, naked, with them. And realized it wasn't so bad at all. In fact, over the years there, I grew to look forward to these shower parties as a time for goofing off, singing into shampoo microphones and slapping each other's butts, but also as a time to come to terms with my body as something as beautiful as all the others. I'd never had a problem seeing my friends' bodies as beautiful: why should mine be different? I worked hard at putting this new idea into fruition. I looked at all the breasts and bellies around me, the pointy, the flat, the round, the mushy, the lopsided, and I loved them. And then I tried to love my own. You know that whole idea of loving yourself before you can love others? It kinda worked the opposite with me and you, Belly. I had to re-remember my love for others' bodies before I could start to love my own, as a sort of forced logic of analogies.

I'm not sure what changed, how these body-math puzzles somehow worked, but slowly, slowly, the roundness, the softness, the lovely fullness of my abdomen seemed a blessing, not an abomination. Listen to the word as you say it to yourself: *Bellllly*. This word, this name, is soft, a soft word for a soft body part. It flows off the tongue, caresses your lips; it is curvy and luscious and soft and sweet. When I'm lying in bed half awake on a sleepy Sunday morning, I run my fingers over you, hum a little song to us of veins and vessels and automobiles, all racing their way across our lovely lump of lower tummy. I am sorry, Belly, that it took so long for me to realize how lovely you are. You are a great friend, the best of the best. You are open and you are kind and you listen, hard, to what I am afraid to say out loud. But you also speak; you give me shit when I deserve it. I love skinny-dipping now as much as you do, am working on speaking out and standing my ground now that me and Mommy don't always see eye to eye. As I've started to listen back, you have quieted. I can currently make out with people sans throw-up, can finish a big test without Pepto Bismol or a sprint to the bathroom. I think that you are now my favorite body part, you poop pranker, you joker you. I am learning to love myself more through loving you.

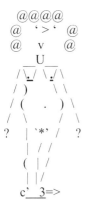

Dear Extra Leg Bone,

It's that time. You're old enough to know: I don't know when you were born.

There. It's out. That's the big secret. I found you one day.

I can't tell you the story of your birth. But I can tell you a story of discovery.

This is that story:
When I was in high school, I played fall soccer. I wasn't very good at soccer, but I was always a decent runner. So in the spring, I ran track, to "stay in shape" for soccer. I wasn't very good at running track either, but that's neither here nor there.

One day, after a workout, we retired to the newly constructed cafeteria. It must have been raining because we usually cooled down and stretched outside. After jogging through the tiled high school halls, we arrived at the food dispensary. We moved the foldable, wheelable, eight to twelve person tables where hundreds of barely post pubescent teens munch on sun chips and sandwiches during the day. We needed room to stretch.

We started stretching in a group circle, led by the captains. The group dynamics deteriorated into small clusters talking and laughing while doing their own calisthenics. I was in a small group, sitting on the tiled floor, doing the butterfly. That's where you hold your ankles with the soles of your feet pressed together and pull them towards your crotch. You can flap your knees like butterfly wings. You get the best stretch if you try to touch your knees to the ground while kissing your feet.

At this point, I don't remember why, I was running my hand along my lower leg. Palm to shin, my thumb felt its way up the calf muscle. When it got to the largest part of the calf, right below the knee, I felt something different. There was a hard bulge where there should only have been flabby muscle.

It felt like bone.

From being a somewhat clumsy runner and kicking myself in the leg, I knew that my right calf bruised easily and took longer to heal than other muscles. Apparently that was your fault.

We went to the doctor together, you and I (and my mother), and found out that you were, in fact, a nub of bone where you shouldn't have been. Apparently, something happened with a growth plate and the bone and while growing, you just, sort of, shot out sideways like a third bulge at the top of the tibia, right before it meets the knee.

It's okay, don't worry about me, the doctor said you're harmless; as long as the muscles around you stay well stretched out.

It's okay, don't worry about you. You're not going anywhere any time soon. I like you, we get along alright, so I'll be keeping you around.

Well, that's it. That's the story of how we discovered one another. Hopefully we'll continue living a fruitful life.

Bye bye now.

Love,
Body

My Darling Thighs,

You met when I was about eleven years old. Seemingly overnight, and certainly without my permission, my girlish body burst forth into womanhood. Suddenly, my face became a battleground of pimples. My hips, formerly known as "the bones connected to my leg bones", transformed into wide, sloping entities unto themselves. My previously flat chest gave way to breasts that would belie my age, and turn gym class into a burden for years to come.

And, in the midst of this chaos, you found each other. You flirted at first, lightly brushing each other during recess. But soon you became inseparable. No matter what I've done since those heady days of puberty ended, you've clung to one another for dear life. You've pushed aside shorts, and worn through denim. Running, yoga, capoeira, and countless squats have left you stubbornly sore, and more enamored of each other than ever.

I admit that over the years, I've held on to some resentment about your relationship. I've been unkind to you. I've tried my best to hide your love. I've devoted quite a lot of time and energy to driving you apart. I've wished you'd disappear. And I've allowed other people to say worse things about you than I've ever imagined.
But I've started to realize that you have the kind of love that lasts a lifetime. And really, who am I to try to tear apart something so beautiful?

I think it's about time we let bygones be bygones. From this day forward, you have my blessing. Touch. Jiggle. Thunder. Do what moves you. You're beautiful, and I love you exactly as you are.

Truly yours,

Attention: People With Body Parts

You coiled beneath the folds
of my stomach
like a spoiled cuss word
I did not know how large and loud
you could get

I remember, in the hospital
wanting to suck all the breath
out of my belly
so that you would leave more quickly

but to tell the truth
I was afraid of you leaving,
like I am always afraid
of what inches of me could be lost
to sterile ruptures
what vulnerable organs
could explode outwards
vanish into pigments
light as history or skin cells

Appendix you are like high school boys and ballet dancing,
I hardly remember you as a wound,
most days.
Most days you are only a thicket of skin,
a fading texture
the half-translucent cobweb
I wear discretely,
like all of my ghosts.

to my blood, wherever you may be,

You've been gone years now, swallowed up in the endless grasses of fields long forgotten. I know it might not be sane that I still think of you, but it's hard when my body won't let me forget. Numb fingers and constant worry; is this what you hoped to leave behind when you left? You see, when I was lying there, wet and sticky with your touch, I realize you took more of me than I can ever completely account for. What I face is more than frustration, but bitterness, hollow in my throat. It does not matter how many attempts I've made to replace you, regardless of the quality of substance. It will never matter, no matter the medication. I was once so strong, so certain, but you made sure to take that away as soon as you left me. Maybe one day I'll find someone who can fill the spaces you left behind, but until then, I'm still thinking about you.

the anemic one

The vaginal shape of the anemone embarrasses me. It is open wide, exposing pink and cavernous depths, not-so-politely *yearning* to be filled to the brim. Standing in the California Academy of Science, I blush and think about you, and my almost-there sex life.

I used to think of tampons and a certain old boyfriend's longest fingers as trespassing and a horrible, not-belonging sensation would creep up through my abdomen. But even with that ugly bile, I longed to be touched and discovered and filled.

But at my first time I was too tense, so the hard pressure of his penis hurt so badly I couldn't stand it. I didn't know how to be open like an anemone, how to invite and engulf a salty warm body into your secret places.

Bleeding from those secret places was horrifying at first, as I thought I had peed my pants in my fifth-grade gym class. But no, I was becoming a woman, and I cried in front of my mother in our bathroom the color of clear ocean water.

"Tampons could make you die," I always thought, reaching for the heavy diaper-like pads instead of the embarrassingly-shaped tubes to be inserted into who knows where, after reading the warnings about toxic shock syndrome on the too-bright-and-too-perky-to-be-about-menstruation boxes.

"Penetration"-what an ugly word…and "intercourse," how…sterile and collegiate—*definitely* not referring to taking a course that counts for credit in two separate departments.

I was afraid of all of these things—the idea that a skin-like strand guarded my virginity and therefore my so-called 'purity' was just plain unhelpful, and made the whole idea of sex scary.

But still, you wanted.

After telling my 16-year-old boyfriend that he could 'go in' with his fingers, some of the dreaded crimson wine was dangled at my lips—so close yet so far--and much too dangerous.

Years later, much more recently, I regard you with wonder.

"Hell yeah!" I say to the V-Day activists with *The Vagina Monologues* and Eve Ensler showing up to support Michigan senators' rights to free speech.

After my first time having intercourse, which was a surprisingly tender and yet animal-like affair, I got the feeling that people don't want me to know what my body is capable of.

They don't want me to know, *society* doesn't want me to know, *the church* doesn't want me to know, that you aren't to be feared, that sex will not instantly destroy me, that blood is not something to hide and tuck behind the old winter sweaters and lost poems in my closet—the body is the body, I am me, and you, though holding court as a powerful temptress as well as merchant of rich crimson silk, are a part of me.

Due respect for you should not be lost, but it should be *gained* by the women and girls who possess it; it is only when I realize the power my body holds and the connecting pieces that link inner worlds to outer worlds, that I am able to more fully appreciate my body as a part of my self. It is not some ghost shell I carry—it has weight and girth and inside places that need more care sometimes than outside places.

Like the heart, you have many chambers of meaning, and must be embraced, and understood, and loved—deeply and purely.

Dear Brain,

Why do you always over think everything and ultimately end up being depressed or full of regret about situations that you took so long to think about in the first place. I take good care of you, I rarely drink, don't smoke, give you medicine when you hurt and this is how you repay me? Get your priorities straight and stop worrying about things that have yet to happen and just go with the flow. I know times are tough in the world, but don't worry about it. If you like someone, don't think about everything that could go wrong. What I'm trying to say is, be more optimistic and something good will happen. You've got to get through all the bad things to get to the good. Keep your head up.

Sincerely,
Me

Leg hair, leg hair,

I sometimes pretend you are fields of restless wheat that outline my home. Unshaven sheep and stray dogs of Lilliput graze around the mole three inches above my right knee. I sometimes see the sun rising between your trenches, your shine catches every ounce of life. Sometimes, I wish you grew into long braids so I could wrap friendship bracelets around every inch of my skin.

Other times: I catch others' glances that loot your home and darken the trenches. The kind that burn my love letters and listen to the flames crack like a fallen branch.

Growing up, everyone undermined you to the long blonde pony-tail that lingered all the way down my back--it was a friendship bracelet I could never attach to my skin. The porcelain doll, they called me. A cross armed, cross legged, carbon copy beauty filed away. One who must never take up space; be touched but not touch. Third grade girls braided your competitor every time Ms. McClure's class watched a movie. Boys, men, reveled in the dripping gold. I remained cross armed, but this time legs uncrossed. Placed in a line up, turned right to left, right to left until guilt fell from my palms. There you were, arrested, barred so close to my skin that you seemed unnatural. I left my shame at your roots, contained in places a porcelain doll should always keep covered.

I betrayed you. Love letters tied to the branches of my deforested legs fell to the ground. At the time, I did not realize you were my nest. My layers upon layers of brown sticks and wheat that made me believe that if I have a nest, I must have wings. I don't belong in this broken shell of a home.

But you were gone.

I sit on the freckled sidewalk miles and years later. You bend in the humid air, bowing down to the grass mingling between the cracks. You, like the grass, would always come back. Through the cracks, through the scar tissue of my razor-cut legs. I trace my fingertips through your misplaced feathers, early mornings, and imperfections. Palms pressed into you like a lover that carves into a tree's bark. Anyone could speculate with distance, but we know that your endless touch means something else, something more.

It means you and I have been close.

Closer than anyone else.

Mustache:

Wax it, bleach it, tweeze it, cream it -- sounds like a Daft Punk song instead of ways to get rid of you, thought nothing changes whenever I succeed. Grudging acceptance of my appearance lasts four, maybe five weeks. Success is momentary in a two front battle. I look at what remains of you and all I see is the forest for the trees; a wildfire's gone through, ripped up some of that soft pink dirt with it, land scabs. Barren. No you, no life forms at all. Always options to weigh: complete annihilation, rip you out by your roots, or just one by one, whoops there goes another rubber tree down. I can't feel the pricking anymore between my eyes, but it's above my lips between my nose ("The septum!" she told me), that still has the capacity to feel pain.

Dear Cancer,

Fuck. You. You have ruined my life. Everything that I have been trying to do with my life had to be fucking put on hold because you decided it was time to start growing. You lined my intestine with yourself and grew. You grew farther in, wider around, and you grew thicker. You taunted me. An unknown pain that grew. My body withered because of you. My fucking self esteem withered because of you. A few extra cells here and there and suddenly all I am is a giant pity party for society. Because of you now everyone can look at me with that pitying look at yours and think, "Oh poor you." I can't stand to look at myself in the mirror because of some extra cells that decided to grow in my intestine. These cells have more power over my life than my own mind. These cells altered my mind, all I can think about is cancer; all I can think about is what if they can't get it all, what if it comes back, what if it keeps growing?

All of my actions come back to this, come back to you. You growing inside me have ruined everything. I can't think, I can't sleep, I can't eat. I can't eat, I can't work, I get tired, I lose weight. I hate myself for losing weight, I hate myself for looking like this, I lose all motivation and self esteem. Thank you for destroying everything that I have been working to create these past two years. In two months you have destroyed me. Single handedly destroyed me. I have struggled so hard to be happy and to make a life for me and with one simple disease I have begun developing these cells that destroy and end lives.

Eyes are always on me now. Once that word is uttered, once that disease is made known to everyone, everything changes. And I just stand that at the center and smile. I crack jokes, I make fun, I plaster on that fake smile. Of course I'm fine. Of course I'll be fine. I just have this stuff growing in me. I just have you growing in me. You. Growing. Widening. Getting stronger. And here I am, just dying. Losing all energy to get by because of this stupid fucking struggle. They tried to burn you all out. They attacked you with everything they thought they needed. Lasers, fire, burning my insides, causing me to bleed profusely. I couldn't stop the bleeding. I just had to sit there, dealing with the pain and discomfort to get you out. Crying every time I walked to far or sat down. Crying when I think about what I'll have to go through for the rest of my life. You are here and you are not going away. But all I want you to do is go away. Just please, go the fuck away... I'm too tired to keep fighting. To keep fighting for the rest of life.

But that's what I have to do. I've been fucking cursed. Cursed with a disease that will always bring you back. That will always bring these cells back to my body. So thanks, I'm sure I'll be seeing you around again.

With Love,
Your Host Body

To the space behind my eyes,

Too many mornings I wake up optimistic and end the day salty and exhausted, pickled in a jar of pain. I try to remember when we were on good terms, before you started to ache. Let me imagine, let me fashion a future together for us that is as peaceful as that almost mythic past. When you first started to hurt other people called me a whiner and I even believed them. But later when you swelled up and burst over my days like the hydrogen bombs over the Pacific Ocean sunrise than there was no space left in me for doubt. During the height there is no thought at all except one, the only important thought, "some day this pain may leave." Medical textbooks and doctors call this migraine with aura. If I had to name it I would call it "The Power and the Glory."

I often return to normal life exhausted, with lingering pain and muscle tension like a bad case of whiplash or head trauma. And I think, "What must I sacrifice to make you healthy?" I've exercised and meditated, taken herbs and supplements, stopped smoking tobacco on any occasion and drinking any more than trivial amounts alcohol or coffee. Since my efforts proceed slowly and fitfully, I try to learn from you. One thing I haven't had to struggle to get: physical pain can hurt *so* much that it causes psychological damage. Or maybe, at their extremes, the two are inseparable, the same thing. What hurts you so much, indefinable space behind my visual feed, sinus canyons and facial bones, can't be contained, it radiates out and hurts all the rest of me.

I try to remind myself that the same principles apply to other people. Suffering spreads between us like a contagion, and as long as it exists to such a horrific degree, it cannot be neatly confined to victims 'other' than ourselves. If this is too depressing, then realize that the same principle works for love, acceptance, and patience. By improving ourselves and working diligently to identify the sources of pain in our own lives, we improve the world in the most real and direct way.

So, little sunspot on my forehead, malfunctioning third eye, I love you. I will do anything to stop your inherited cycles of convulsive pain, and I know that someday I will find a medication or diet which will at least reduce the symptoms to a manageable level. Until then I wait patiently, and try to understand how people's faces and eyes can hide so much pain.

Dear Brain

Gray folds, ridges and valleys:
I feel your muted throbbing
against my skull walls
and I know you are a dammed lake—
yoked down by your own
colossal weight—you want freedom.

But without me, gray folds,
you would spill
through ridges and valleys
faucets and streams,
spread so thin
that you forget your own name.
So I must keep you
captive for now.

Dear Anus,

You and I have been through a lot. I put you through a lot of shit, and you take that shit. I just really like food, and well, the delicious food does not always make you the happiest, but I just feel that your unhappiness is outweighed by my tongues pleasures. I guess it is probably not fair to value your happiness less than that of the other body parts.

That was greatly recognized by your most recent protest. The doctor says it was probably viral, but I know it was you just being a real asshole. We are twenty-two years old now, and I guess you have an expectation for me to meet certain nutritional qualifications with my meals. Now in my defense, it was really, really hot that day. The rest of the body all agreed that ice cream for dinner was a great idea! You were simply outvoted. My body is a democratic dicktatorship. We try for everyone's opinions to be considered, but the majority usually rules unless y'know, a lady is involved. So I just wanted to be clear, your message was received. The rest of us will try our best to give you fiber and vegetables and other nutrients for dinner. For God's sake though, don't give us another 5 day shit-in protest!

-Brain

P.S. Get ready for the county fair, I hear they have more deep fried butter!

"Hey, beautiful! Damn, look at those eyes."
"She's got these giant bug-eyes, like a frog freak."
"Wow, blue is really your color. Look how it matches your eyes!"
"You've got Stone eyes. You look just like your mother."

I found an ink drawing of my mother at twenty-three years old, her face tilted slightly upward toward the artist, angry and alarmed gaze warning the viewer that she was both dangerous and terribly vulnerable the summer I was sixteen. It terrified me that my mother, whom I had always suspected of being depressed or somehow deeply unsatisfied, could look at herself like this in the mirror for as long as it must have taken her to complete the self-portrait. What an arresting look, the look of someone driven into taking herself very seriously. The look of someone who has both seen a ghost and killed a man. What terrified me more was that I recognized that look in her eyes as my own.

Because you have always been my most distinctive and recognizable feature, often the way I am identified to people who don't know me well, orb-eyes of mine, you have become masters of emotional espionage. *Come here!* you cry sometimes, arms flailing over the starboard railing of a sea liner. *Get the fuck away from me*, you flare. I can laden you easily with pain, the muscle memory of my skin and nerves bending cells readily into that old forlorn formation. This seems connected to the constant feeling that I take in more of the world than most people, that more fits through my retinas and completes the quest to my memory. You snap up every mood, every movement, every neurosis and utterance, every shift in temperament or social dynamic, and file it away for further analysis. Is your largeness, your otherness away from the rest of my face and body, the reason I unintentionally cram so much into my mental spread sheets of other people's minds? Seems mystical, literary, the idea that one's appearance reflects one's inner self, and the luxury of glorifying the self is one I sometimes cannot resist. Am I a Seer, will you grow milky and clouded in old age when I have seen enough to see what is next? I think this would be all right.

Attention: People With Body Parts

Stomach

All my life I yearned for your smallness
for your tapering away into
rib-cage and muscle
I wanted you a flat balloon
incapable of floating or flying
I wanted you to hold no
blood or babies
I wanted you hard and unforgiving
as mothers or pavement
I wanted no head
to find rest in your folds
you stay slick-taut as
the sails of a dying ship
you breathe quietly,
you stay low.

Dear Nose,

I remember the day I first started to dislike you. I was in middle school, with a basically neutral image of self, and the family and I were dropping my sister off at soccer camp. I was idling by the car and just happened to catch a glimpse of my profile reflected in the window and I remember thinking, "*That's* what I look like? But I'm *ugly*!"

You see, I was used to seeing you head on. Looking normal. Perhaps you were never model-esque, but you were a nice nose, even, I was a little proud to think, a unique one. And I liked your freckles. But with that sudden paradigm shift, I was shocked by what I now refer to as your "elegant curve." Your tip seemed too pointy, nostrils long and thin. A nose fit more for a 90's cartoon witch or, worse, a rat.

With the realization that I might truthfully be ugly, the years that followed were an attempt to arrive at a solid conclusion. Every time I walked past a reflective surface-mirrors, windows, puddles of water (yes, actually), occasionally spoons-I would evaluate my reflection: Ugly? Not ugly? I scoured every photograph of myself I could get my hands on, and for a proper scientific comparison examined them in relation to photographs of my friends. Throughout all of this, I paid particular attention to you, and how you harmonized (or, more often, didn't) with the rest of my face. I remember pushing down on the bridge of my nose in the hopes that consistent application of pressure would bend you into a more linear and aesthetically-pleasing shape. I'm sorry about that.

Thankfully, that phase was short lived along with my thoughts on getting plastic surgery. For the most part, the worst of my negative body image was fading by the time I entered college. I'm not exactly sure why, it just started to ebb on it's own. Perhaps I simply grew tired of trying to quantify myself, and you, as being either acceptable or abhorrent multiple times a day.

The decision to get you pierced was a big one. I had believed nose rings to be very attractive, elegant and sophisticated for quite some time, however there was a piece of me that was still hesitant to adorn you, to ornament and draw attention to you through jewelry. Getting that first stud was painful, but also thrilling. I was catching my reflection in car windows again, but in a positive way. When that piercing rejected, after 11 months of dealing with chronic infections, I was frustrated with you again. I was angry at my immune system for being overly sensitive, and I was angry at you. I realized later that the fault, of course, was mine, and the improper way I was cleaning your piercing.

The other day, I was listening to a friend's grandmother tell her story. She had a visa that allowed her to cross from Turkey to America, and she came to get a nose job. While here, she met her husband, married and settled down to raise her family. The whole course of her life changed, because of her nose. Listening, I was reminded of the power that we give to our negative perceptions of ourselves, and how much that can shape our lives. Though it's a relatively rare day when I have negative thoughts about you, sometimes it still happens. A friend will take a "bad" photograph of me, or I'll compare myself to another friend. However, I try to brush those thoughts aside. I remember that you are kin to my own grandmother's nose-she died before I was born, but I am told that we are very similar in looks and personality-and I like to think of you as a tangible, visible, physical link to my family and my history.

Your new stud is healing nicely. I can't wait to exchange it for a ring, and I hope that as the hours, days and months pass by our relationship continues to grow fonder.

Dear Hair,

I hope you know how much I appreciate you. You usually fall just the way I want you to, I can style you and shape you and do wonderful things with you. Not to mention how great you are at putting up with all the dye and chemicals. When I need you to, you take in all the dye and shine with vibrant purples and blues that make the world jealous. Needless to say, I love you.

Well.

I only love you when you stay on the top of my head. But then you start to wander. You wander down my face and across my chin, sliding over my lip. Then I start to dislike you. Then you shatter my illusion of androgyny and my feeling of beauty. I hope you don't take it personally when I shave you off. Frequently. But it's with love I promise. Because you are still perfect when you are on top of my head.

But then you still wander.

You wander under my arms, down my chest, around my nipples and down my stomach. Your reaches extend to unmentionable areas as you continue to wrap your way down my body till you reach my ankles. And you don't even stop there, you manage to wiggle your way just a little bit farther till you have a small patch growing right on top of my foot. Do you know how annoyed that makes me? Drives me insane every time I see it.

Yet I still try to love you and focus on the positives of you. Focus on the luscious locks that flow from my head in pretty colors. And think happy thoughts as I spray my body with chemicals to cease your growth. Slide razors up, down, around, and all over to trim you down. All in the name of beauty and self esteem.

You know, the growth rate of you and my self esteem are pretty negatively related. As you grow, my self esteem drops, but as you shrink my self esteem grows. If only I could just contain you to own location. The top of my head. That's where you always make me happy. You can stand up high in a proud Mohawk. You can sway in the breeze when you are down. And you just give off that androgynous illusion that I try to embody every day.

As much trouble as you give me, I can only say that I appreciate everything you do. And if I have to continue my life with an endless stock of razors to keep this beautiful colored mop perfect, then I guess I will have to. Though just know, if there ever comes a cheaper way to end your growth spreading across my body, I will probably invest in it. God knows these razor bumps can get irritating all the time. And I would quite enjoy not having to shave off that happy trail every other day. Or my legs. Or my ass. Or my junk. Or my armpits. I mean, a little of you is okay. But god, you need to just hold your roll on your growing patterns. A man can only afford so many razors.

Signed with love.

Dear ovaries

I can never properly convey my feelings towards you. I try and try but the words become mixed in the whirlpool of my thoughts. I give up and let your influence sink into the abyss. But like a never forgotten ex, you come back.

Before pcos you were like the acquaintance I friended a long time ago. I would forget you existed or at least I tried. But you would remind me of your presence with a loud and obnoxious status update that was difficult to ignore.

After the doctors verdict you are the book I cannot close. You both are a part of me. A part of my body, the influence to my mind, and the decider to my future offspring.

Like an angry lion there are ways to control you. I can temper down your rage with magical pills. But to sooth you it must be done every day. If I escape from the magic, than I surely will pay.

My mind is a ball of yarn because of you. The more I try to untangle it, the more knots I make. A pouty child, I sit on the floor in despair. I do not want to take more magical pills. But I crave the sword that will slash these thoughts from my mind.

In that whirlpool of my thoughts there are a few exotic animals of thought. It swishes and swirls in my mind. Everything in my life is a variable. But I thought children were the one constant. Never mind the significant other aspect of the story. That is another chapter. He too will come to understand this whirlpool.

You are like family. As much as I wish you were not here, you are and you plan to stay. Sometimes you create noise and pain and I have to console you with more pills. I nervously wait every month for the visit. I wait for the pain and treat it as it goes. I worry and wait for the future.

In the end I cannot wish you gone. I am an unfinished house with this whirlpool of thoughts and I am only beginning to pick up the hammer to nail these words together.

Lots of love

My Butt

Anyone who's taken an introductory physics class knows that force equals mass times acceleration. If a car hits you at sixty miles an hour, it's not going to feel good. If a kitten hits you at sixty miles an hour, then that's one fast kitten. I have a tiny butt, but I hear that my butt is cute, no if, ands or buts about it. Also, my butt has a lot of force when I use it to dance. Welcome to the story about my butt.

I was born in Texas and for the majority of my life I didn't think about my butt. They say that everything is bigger in Texas but this definitely wasn't the case with my butt. The fact of the matter was that my butt didn't have significant meaning in my life. Occasionally I would fall down and think, "Ouch, that hurts." He would say to me, "suck it up man!" That was about the extent of the interaction with him, however, things would soon change when I traveled to the far land of the east coast for school.

Going to school out of state forced me to grow up quickly. I had to make friends or college would consume me. Fortunately, I developed two key techniques for making friends in college, even those I was unaware of these techniques. The first was listening by nodding my head quickly, vigorously and in all directions. I could have written an article about my forehead, but it's too easy of a target because I have a five-head unlike most people.

After I broke up with my girlfriend from Texas, you soon came into play. I had adopted the notorious party boy dance technique in high school, but I decided to mix it up in college. You were out of control on the dance floor! I booty bumped people, dropped it low, brought it back up, shook you round and round, and made a fool of myself. You would convince me to keep going and I would say, "okay, but just this one time mister." Somehow it all worked and I have a girlfriend now, hurray!

Today I use you often, mainly for sitting at work. Even

though you still don't come into play much I can think of scenarios where it could come into play as listed below.

- A shark would never eat me because my butt is simply too small and cute
- I can use my butt only when I need it, and you know when that is
- My butt doesn't come up with excuses, only results
- In sentences I can easily make puns with the word but and butt
- I always have something to fall back on, on my butt
- "I didn't mean to butt in but butts are great!"- my butt

To my hips,

You don't exist. At least that's what my mom says, do you remember what she calls me sometimes? The hipless wonder. I hope you're not insulted. The first time she did was years ago, after I fit into that prom dress the shop owner wouldn't even let me try on. "It won't work," she'd said. But you made it happen, you and your lack of existence. So even if you were hurt by what my mom said, you shouldn't be. In the best way, you defy practicality.

There's a number out there, .7, that stands for the perfect hip-to-waist ratio for the female species. I think that means that if you have a twenty-four inch waist and your hips measure 34, you are perfect. You are a woman. My hips, you don't make the cut. You're boyish, you don't count as curves. You fall straight in line with my waist. Because of you, or because you're not there, I can wear patterned trousers and baggy jeans. I can belt a garbage bag and declare it a dress, if I felt like it. The world of fashion tells me this is good; so do my friends with some shape in the bottom half of their bodies. But they have something real to hold onto and to stuff into wrap dresses and I have you, my bones, and boy's clothing.

For the longest time, I was the only one that really knew you were there. You hid somewhere between my legs and my boobs (I was only given so much to make me a woman; I think my boobs took all of it). You were always covered by gathered skirts and oversized sweaters. But I could feel you; when I lay flat on my back you were two mountains whose sharp peaks felt urgent against my hands. I could feel you shift under my muscles and veins, could feel how you would strain to support my stomach that stretched out flat between you (it was mostly flat but sometimes it puffed out and you hide in shame, or it was concave and you emerged even more, victorious). I would trace you and grip you with both hands, trying to imagine how you feel to someone who hasn't grown up with you not growing.

I imagine you feel surprising, and unexpected. There's spine up there, taking up all the attention in its knobby fascination, so readily felt through back rubs or sexually tense hugs, when I'd deliberately angle you backwards and our bodies would form a lumpy Eiffel Tower. It would take some extra flirting, or eye contact, or maybe a beer for that form to straighten out, for someone to take notice of you. You might feel fragile and small but you might hurt someone too, if you're pressed hard enough against someone else, at the right angle. I like that about you, hips. You're a conveniently stealth weapon.

I wonder if you hurt him, the one who I'll call September. By the time he came along, there were a handful of people out there who would've been made aware of your existence. You'd been gripped by hands that weren't mine, pressed into objects that weren't my mattress, that were other, living people. This one, September, would've noticed you, all right. He could tell you were there; he said even though he thought I had an ugly face he'd do it again because he was into the anorexic look. You must've been looking particularly sharp that night. I kind of hope you caused him pain, but maybe that's what he likes about the anorexic look. Being able to really feel what he's hurting.

Since those years in which you were supposed to show up but didn't, I've worked to prove you're there. You're not wide enough to be womanly. If I shrunk my waist and stretched my cells thin enough to let you emerge, I thought maybe you might start to look like you actually exist. But you remember what happened; the other players in the woman trifecta, boobs and period, up and quit in protest. There wasn't enough of me left to sustain all of you. The anorexic look was turning me into a child again, stripping me of any woman I had left. That scared me, so I'm letting you recede a bit. You might get less attention, you might not cause as much pain, but I imagine that might be a relief. Anybody who finds you now will have taken the trouble to really look.

I hope that feels good to you, because it does to me. You know you can be noticed without struggling to break through my skin, and I'm done wrecking myself to give you a chance in the spotlight. Whatever covers you now I see as sheltering, not obstructing you. If everything looks a bit softer now it's because I'm ready to loved, really loved, and I'll make sure you don't have to protect me from the people I let feel you. The knives have been, so to speak, sheathed, and we'll be one person from now on. Your role as protector to my victim can retire.

I think you felt that change, the last time. This one was different; when he held you he wasn't just touching you, he was touching me and you're a part of me. He didn't cut me up into ugly face/good body/bony hips, but talked about me like I was already complete. He wasn't holding my parts together, but just holding me and it was nice to fall asleep like that. He noticed you without noticing you; noticed your lack without thinking of it as a lack.

Neither do I, anymore. Sometimes, I resent you, but it's nothing to do with how far you stick out from my stomach. You're not going to make it easy for me to give birth. Sex hurts sometimes because there's just not a whole lot of room down there. But you let me squeeze through small spaces and fit between large people on airplanes. Boys jeans are comfortable and I thank you for helping me wear them. I like that you're flexible even though you pop more than necessary, just to remind me that you're there.

I hope I can find a pair of hands to hold you like you matter. I hope they'll be attached to someone who will look at me like I matter more than anything. You carry a lot of my history around with you; I hope someone will rest their hands on your curves long enough for me to say it all to them one day, and not remove them when I'm done. And it's going to hurt, but one day you're going to have the responsibility to carry my children around, and get them out into the world when they're ready. And if one of them is another hipless wonder, you and I are going to show her that she's lucky.

A short note to my thighs

When the separation of brain and body first took place,
When my mother's flaws found unwelcome roots in my budding
flesh,
You came to me, not as a blessing, but
As a deformity

Like weeds who drown out the potential,
Who squelch the cultivation of a newborn seedling,
So that simple maturity, the confidence to grow,
Is told again and again that it cannot be

A relationship that was not mine,
Between my mother and her growing vines
Her unchangeable, torturous feeling that
Her thighs were too large, too raw, too fat

Came to me, a soliloquy
That the thighs she spoke of appeared to be
Of the same shape and quality
As the ones that were attached to me

The lines we had we did not see
In the long, narrow chutes of magazines:
The ones that tell you
What you will never be

No seedling now, as I am grown
Left in a fight that was not my own
But now it is my struggle to bear
Fearing judgment, a passing glare

From passersby who might notice me
Not for brain or passion or plea
But for the thighs my family sees:
Too large, too raw, too fat

Yet the enemy is intertwined
A cord of hate from my mother's vine
Became a slicing voice inside of me
Clinging to a woven history

Attention: People With Body Parts

To let that go is what I seek,
To escape generational legacy
For deliverance from a broken vision
Of my body that cannot be
Yet the morning mirror always repeats
The chant, "too fat" that tethers me
A family story with sunken teeth
Tangled roots, on-going grief

So here is to liberation, yours is mine.
But how?

To my hymen:

Ripped out, you push me in.
You push me deep into my skin.

You seal me off from the love in lovers' hands. They will detach
you from this skin. They will see me as a sunken body and see
you as the epitome of my personhood, regardless of my legs that
can run on lonely pavement or my fingers that can scratch bare
backs until he understands the meaning of no. This is based upon
the assumption that his hands are every man's hands.

You cradle all of my insecurities. You carry stories and echo
screams of "He is coming back"
       Back
   Back
         Back
until it fades into silence.

You push me deep into my skin.
Your pain will always come back: the first man that touched you
pushed you back into a corner, and made you black and blue.
He pushed me deep into my skin. So. Deep.
I feel responsible--you lost a body that you can never grow back.
You are now unsealed, and bore with holes for nightmares to
sink into your folds.

It's coming back. It's coming back. In the fingerprints of my next
lover, there are no life lines. There is only evidence that
someone else was here Pushing, pushing,
Pushing.
I catch my breath.

Pushing.

He is in so deep. So deep, there is no more room in my skin for
me.

To my skin—

It's no secret that I have been disappointed in you most of my life. You are:
1. Too pale (rosy cheeks and freckles don't count.)
2. Too susceptible to being burnt by the sun, probably because of #1.
3. Too ticklish in weird places. Why not just the bottoms of my feet? Why also that strip of skin above my pubic bone? When people hug me, or travel their hands around my waist, I will erupt in giggles and twitches…SO TICKLISH. BAH.

I know that you are just proof of my heritage from my English, Scottish, and German ancestors, the people who lived high in the northlands, where the sun rarely shone. I know, I know, it's how my genes are. But still…I have never been able to tan, or even freckle completely for a faux-tan, and so therefore have never been like the beach beauties with their tans and laying out in the sun for hours. I never have been able to wear the colors yellow and green quite like tan people do. I know it's super self-centered of me, but still, it hasn't been easy. I've been so self-conscious about bathing suits, about my pale legs that Jake called "chicken legs" way back in second grade, about being fairly luminescent in the bright sun. I get all pink when I'm hot and it gets kind of ridiculous, breaking out in hives sometimes, though not as bad as mom does.

But still, we've been a lot of places together. We've been to Europe, we've been to Lake Michigan, we've been under different people's hands as they touch that oh-so-tender spot below my belly. Sometimes I think about those times with that one guy, yeah, you know who I'm talking about. You loved being touched by him, the way he ran his hands all over you, and I'm talking ALL OVER YOU, so tender and caring, but so firm, so that we knew that he wanted me. I've thought that if is lips were hot coals or flame, you would be burned to a crisp because of all the places he placed his mouth. I'd feel all burned up, with nothing to show for it except for some purple bruises on my neck.

You took it really hard, that time at the beach when I did try, I really did try hard, to wear and reapply sunscreen but I guess it just didn't take--and then suddenly you were all burned and buckling and bubbling like you were actually some kind of sauce that was covering my bones and muscles. Like I had been heated over a stove too long and was bubbling over, or that I cooked a little too long like the Christmas ham that sometimes gets little bumps before the skin breaks and cracks into thin sheets. *I didn't want to be that ham.* But mom took care of me well, spraying aloe all over me so that her hands didn't touch you and hurt me worse. I wore baggy clothes, and looked like a gangsta for the part of July that I was letting you rest from the sun. After that, I swore that I'd never get burned again. I used to resist sunscreen like the devil, but now I embrace it like some crazy person so cancer won't get you. I wish I could hook up an IV so that protection could just be channeled to you permanently.

I'm sorry, I really am sorry.

And this business of feeling comfortable in my own skin—I get more comfortable with you as the years go on. I am learning to love you, learning to be comfortable with the way you stretch over my thighs and fold over my elbows, the way that you tenderly cover my bones and sinews and muscles and blood. Though I don't have all of the plump curves of a Rubinesque vixen, I am convinced that you are as delicate and pearly as such.

Your freckles make patterns, have you ever noticed that? Do they tickle? Does it feel silly when more pop out after I spend considerable time in the sun, or when a new hair pops out of the moles on my arms? Does it hurt when I get slivers and scratches? Do you like me to wear shoes outside or are you invigorated by the feeling of grass and dirt and sand and roots beneath my feet? Or what about when I dance barefoot and my blisters and calluses get so thick that I could cut them off—does that hurt or are you willing to sacrifice something for such a wonderful endeavor as dancing? Do I keep you too cold or too hot, do you actually like wool and cashmere and it's all in my head? Do you actually *crawl* when I get chilled or nervous? Because I imagine you move all over my body like a conveyor belt—the skin on my knee now covering my right shoulder.

You are so soft and warm and smooth, and you've been

complimented so many times for being that way.

I'm glad you're mine.
    I'm glad we are together,
    And I believe I am learning to appreciate you for who you are—
    That is,
    Part of me.

Love,

me

watch my hands guide you to her deathbed
watch my hands drawn splinter and blood
watch my hands glide under poetry
watch my hands follow around and inside her
watch me watch my hands

I have these hands; I want you to have crept anywhere they were welcome. In a way, everything begins with you, the extensions out on the edge, on the verge of grasping something wonderful. I know that some good can come of you; miles of specifics lie in the way.

I'm used to physical exhaustion; I only know from family and lovers what it's like to lose one's grip, when the body won't respond. I certainly fight with my body as a transperson, but I'm still of its strong hands, ready for production. I'm positioned to productivity as part of my whiteness, and of the upper-middle class narrative of hard work (always in the safest of circumstances) becomes wealth (i.e. value). Work is only a step to value, necessarymeaningless. My uncle tried to argue me an American Meritocracy at dinner; I smiled, refused to sit with him, and did dishes for my grandmother instead. Even in this, though, I'm relying on the system of approved symbols that my body relies on, the state climaxing and reproducing continuously in my hands. I'm also depressive/chronically anxious, which means to me that the highest stakes are always riding on the value of what my hands do. This has wore on me, and I have not slept.

With that, you are where my violence lives. I can't reason myself out of it, though sometimes I can lead myself away. Racing thoughts at the apex of stress become wracking full-body twitches that I only barely understand: gestures of thought becoming twisted fantasies, which then explode; a start-stop release of all desire to cause pain; an explosion generated and contained to keep peace. The twitches start at my core, and held back bring me to fetal, but I think that if I ever lost control it would begin with you, losing a grip, submitting unto another...every fantasy of destruction that anger's given me.

You're banal too. I get lost to the logic of my carpentry, the dance with wood, the most relaxed I can be. You are trained and retrained to know how to follow its touch, do it best, such that it not only looks easy but has become, with miles of history behind them, easy. It's part protestant work ethic, part water and chopped wood; at its best I reclaim labor. But I usually exit my wood-trances with new marks everywhere, the consequences of experience, the fruits of losing oneself. Intention is irrelevant.

Pain and me, we hang out. I like pain. I'm certainly kinky, but also nonsexually masochistic. An easy explanation: I will you to self injury from what my body's learned being depressive and trans and under various logics of capitalism...but that doesn't account for how I've been otherwise privileged, and as work it doesn't fit the progress narrative that "reclaiming" so often implies. Nobody's fighting for healthy whole-hearted cutters. You tell me on top of a knife blade tell me "There's nothing easy."

Sex is honestly easier to talk about, as a performance, a narrative. Sex feels like craft to me, the stable peace of knowing what my hands can do for a body. You have strong fingers but weak wrists, so when I'm fingering someone I can't lie next to them without pain and loss of endurance. My posture becomes perpendicular, breeding distance and terrible quiet in expectation of a coming orgasm, an influence which I'm not yet strong enough to overcome. I remember the first time I fisted someone, finishing, feeling the stick on you, and as he lays me back I see blood everywhere. "That's normal," he says, and he's right. I reflect on the coagulating blood on my still-clenched hand as he fucks me. But other times entirely I'm lying softly next to someone and I'm fingering Chopin on their back. We can be romantic and clean and open-eared together.

There are lots of ways to make music, but I'm a piano player. I have large hands. I've learned a bunch of other instruments; in doing so, in building new polyphony and habit into muscle memory, one changes the contours of the brain. "Lobe-interconnection" my piano teacher used to tell me over Bach. The head tries to keep up with the hands, or so often vice versa, each in their element, the not-quite-neutral flesh and every unnatural miraculous thought. The balance these is mediated and unresolved in the moving of hands, the disturbing the space.

I live a religion of wood, ivory, skin, and steel, and I'm terrified I can't pray without these palms. Every mark on my body, my beloved armor, my book of myself, my living story, is written underneath some pen that I wielded. I hope, with all the world my hands have learned, to continuing unravelling myself from you, to always build with my heart as my hands untangle, to love myself aware that any second for me, and already for others, you'll fail.

   you hold me close
   with my hands tied behind my back
   building faith in something
   I have that my hands
   can't give.

Attention: People With Body Parts

My body was made to be with other bodies.
These ribs were made for hands to hold
Each groove humming
Reaching fingers sliding into gear
My abdomen is a resting place for wind-blown cheeks
Knuckles to be kissed by thorough lips
My clavicle to be nipped in lazy tired violence
Teeth to bump shyly against other teeth
Toe-nails to trace the curves
of legs unformulated

Attention: People With Body Parts

Epilogue

This book is a testament to the myth of the great body-mind divide.

A body is an audience, a vessel of histories, a muscle memory of life. It carries a first kiss and the wounds from lost opportunities. Sometimes it is even responsible for such losses. These are the body parts that make it so difficult to sign a letter with love. The body parts we detach from out of shame or reinforcement, the ones that plague our spirit and make some wish the body could divide from the mind. I wish I could reassure that World War Me is over, love. No body part belongs in a landfill or deserves to be filled with land mines.

The next time you pause before signing a letter to your body with love, remember what is yours. Your body is yours. It is filled with so much movement it collides with others. It is so powerful it produces music and babies that are whole.

Most days are filled with opportunities our body gives us. The moments that establish a foundation for all of the beautiful things we build. Speak to your body, write to it, indulge with extra sprinkles and use it as fairy dust.

It is there and we are here, undivided.

Attention: People With Body Parts

BodyMind:Undivided

This grand list of tips, tricks, and activities originated as a Google Document shared with everyone involved in the making of *Attention: People With Body Parts*. This continues to act as an inspirational space for folks deciding which body part to write to and those who struggle to find their alignment between the body/mind.

Please note that not every suggestion on this list is a safe or viable option for every body

1. Have someone trace out outline of your body with sidewalk chalk or marker
2. Stretch
3. Take close up photos of random parts of your body   (a patch of skin on your leg, the inside of your ear, etc). Study them.
4. Go a day without speaking
5. Listen to Andrea Gibson
6. Watch *Seven Pounds* and/or *Wit*
7. Take a bath
8. Eat slowly
9. Sleep outside, preferably somewhere textured
10. Collage
11. Make a list of safe spaces. Visit them if possible
12. Sex--the good kind
13.This: www.theinspirationblog.net/showcases/30-amazing-examples-of-creative-body-paint-art/ (sorry a majority of them

are female bodied)

14. Hold your breath
15. Listen to someone else's heartbeat or your own
16. Alter your shaving schedule
17. Close your eyes more often
18. Sweat
19. Laugh out loud, but like actually
20. Look at old pictures of yourself: how has your body changed?
21. Wear clothes you really like, and clothes you've never tried...wear someone else's clothes!
22. Dance
23. Hang out with animals; try to get on their level
24. Sing
25. Change up your relationship with the mirror (have a meditative session with it, or go a week without it)
26. Start with a part of your body and write stream-of-consciousness of some memories that come to mind when you think of it
27. Look for your reflection in unusual surfaces (moving cars, dark computer screens, a puddle, etc)
28. Lay flat on your stomach or back without moving
29. Lay next to someone else without moving
30. Get naked and put on some music that makes you feel like a superstar
31. Make faces at babies. Use your facial muscles!
32. Make faces at yourself - make faces at strangers!
33. Documentary: *America the Beautiful*
34. Take off all your clothes (a la Nelly) and do some naked yoga
35. Donate blood and learn more about the impact of organ donors
36. invent a sport
37. Jump in a moon bounce and become weightless
38. Find your favorite place to play the body-drums (I am especially fond of the lower-belly-chest combo)
39. Master the art of shadow puppets, using your whole body and not just your hands
40. Draw a face on different parts of your body--the face it would make if you were to have a conversation with it. Leave the markings there for at least one day

41. Count the number of times you perform some mundane action over a span of time...number of throat clearings in a day, nail bites in a class, etc.

42. RadioLab: An hour dedicated to stories of the mind-body link
http://www.radiolab.org/2006/may/05/

43. Play connect-the-dots with your moles and freckles

44. Go vegan for a week

45. Play an instrument until your hands feel sore and blistered

46. Shovel dirt or do other manual labor for a few hours and feel how good it is to use your body!

47. Don't shower for a week or a month

48. Allow a part of your body to fall asleep and feel all the tingling sensations

49. Play in the dirt, or better yet, in the mud

50. Cry

51. Smile so much it hurts

52. Frown

53. Laugh til your abs are sore

54. Give yourself a scalp massage

55. Give yourself a jaw massage

56. Rub your temples (lightly)

57. Rub your sinuses (along your brow bone and down along your nose)

58. Swing on a swing set with your eyes shut

To see the continuation of this list, please visit the *Attention: People With Body Parts'* official website.

Attention: People With Body Parts

Attention: People With Body Parts

About this guy

Lexie Bean is a writer and activist working on her degree in Idealism from Oberlin College.

ATTENTION: PEOPLE WITH BODY PARTS, her first published project, is only the starting point for her continued work to create body-positive spaces through intersectional approaches and the arts.

Please visit www.attentionpeoplewithbodyparts.org if you have interest in…

- learning more about the project
- collaborating!
- writing to a body part / reading more
- adding your own wisdom to the BodyMind: Undivided List
- saying hello (in English, French, Hungarian, or Danish!)